THE BATTLE OF FRIBOURG 1644

Enghien and Turenne at War

Stéphane Thion

'This is the Century of the Soldier', Fulvio Testi, Poet, 1641

HELION & COMPANY

Helion & Company Limited
Unit 8 Amherst Business Centre
Budbrooke Road
Warwick
CV34 5WE
England
Tel. 01926 499 619
Email: info@helion.co.uk
Website: www.helion.co.uk
X, formerly Twitter: @helionbooks
Visit our blog https://helionbooks.wordpress.com/

Published by Helion & Company 2024
Designed and typeset by Mary Woolley, Battlefield Design (www.battlefield-design.co.uk)
Cover designed by Paul Hewitt, Battlefield Design (www.battlefield-design.co.uk)

Text © Stéphane Thion 2024
Photographs and illustrations © as individually credited
Front cover colour artwork by Marco Capparoni © Helion and Company 2024
Maps by George Anderson © Helion and Company 2024

Every reasonable effort has been made to trace copyright holders and to obtain their permission for the use of copyright material. The author and publisher apologize for any errors or omissions in this work and would be grateful if notified of any corrections that should be incorporated in future reprints or editions of this book.

ISBN 978-1-804515-51-8

British Library Cataloguing-in-Publication Data.
A catalogue record for this book is available from the British Library.

All rights reserved. No part of this publication may be reproduced, stored in a retrieval system, or transmitted, in any form, or by any means, electronic, mechanical, photocopying, recording or otherwise, without the express written consent of Helion & Company Limited.

For details of other military history titles published by Helion & Company Limited contact the above address or visit our website: http://www.helion.co.uk.

We always welcome receiving book proposals from prospective authors.

Contents

Introduction: European political context at the beginning of 1644   v

1	The 1644 campaign	9
2	Commanders	21
3	The French Army in 1644	28
4	The Bavarian army	46
5	Preamble: 28 July 1644	55
6	The Attack by the Duc d'Enghien, 3 August 1644	63
7	The Second Battle (5 August 1644)	77
8	Epilogue	92
	Conclusion	95
	Colour Plate Commentaries	100

Appendices:
I	Order of 10 October 1642	106
II	Extract from the order of 20 December 1643	113
III	Typical deployment of an army in 1644	114
IV	An army in battle in 1644	116

Bibliography   118

The author would like to extend a special thank you to Stephen Ede Borrett for his work on this project.

Introduction

European political context at the beginning of 1644

With the deaths of Richelieu and Louis XIII in 1642 and 1643, French strategy appeared to be on hold. Richelieu's plan for Louis XIII had always been 'to halt the progress of Spain.'[1] In 1633, the Cardinal-Duc warned the King to take care that France would not have to bear a defensive war alone against Spain and the Empire. It was therefore imperative for him to maintain the Dutch and Swedish alliances. Fortunately for France, Jules Mazarin, Richelieu's successor, adopted this strategy. Father Bougeant describes Mazarin as:

> less vindictive than his predecessor, but less benevolent, almost equally insensitive to insults and services; misery even in his generosity; timid, trembling at the approach of a disgrace, but firm and patient in the disgrace itself, even more skilful at rising from it, proposing to yield in order to regain more advantage.

But above all he was an excellent negotiator:

> as he had spent his whole life in negotiations, he knew, so to speak, all the finesses of the art. The dispatches he sent to the French plenipotentiaries in Münster are always clear, specious and well reasoned; one can admire in them an extraordinary skill backed up by tireless work to ensure the success of affairs.[2]

This transfer of power worried the Swedes, who had been France's allies since the beginning of the war. Mistrust was all the greater because, in the letter that the Queen Regent sent to Queen Christina of Sweden after the victory at Rocroi, no mention was made of the treaty of alliance between the two

---

1 Armand J. du Plessis de Richelieu, *Mémoires du Cardinal de Richelieu,* in Nouvelle Collection des Mémoires pour Servir à l'Histoire de France (Paris: Michaud & Poujoulat, 1838), tome VII, p.576.
2 Guillaume Hyacynthe Bougeant, *Histoire des Guerres et des Négociations qui précédèrent le traité de Westphalie* (Paris: Jean Mariette, 1727), p.516.

Cardinal Mazarin by Pierre Mignard (Musée Condé, via Wikipedia Commons)

countries. The Swedes therefore asked France for clarification, and a deed confirming the last treaty of alliance was sent from Paris on 20 June 1643 and signed by the Queen of Sweden on 28 July of the same year.

Peace negotiations began at the end of 1644 and led to the signing of the Treaties of Westphalia in 1648. Until 1643, the various Catholic and Protestant parties had not seen fit to meet. That year, two cities were chosen as the venue for the talks: Münster and Osnabrück. The Holy Roman Empire, Spain, France and the United Provinces negotiated in Münster, while the Empire and Sweden did the same in Osnabrück. In July 1643, negotiations were slow to get underway, with each negotiator fearing, 'either to appear to desire peace too much, or to expose himself to the sort of shame that comes from waiting a long time for those with whom one must deal'.[3] The Emperor's plenipotentiaries were the first to go to the venue, wishing to demonstrate their desire to find a peaceful solution to the conflict, but the other parties involved were less eager. The Spanish simulated the same diligence as their ally, while at the same time trying to instil a strong mistrust of the French in the Swedes. Queen Christina, for her part, wanted to convince her French allies that she would not deal with them independently, while at the same time showing her zeal to bring about peace. The French, for their part, promised that they would arrive in Münster on 1 January 1644, a promise they would not keep.[4] The Queen and Mazarin wanted to confirm the peace treaty with the United Provinces before entering into any negotiations. It would take some time for this plan to come to fruition, with numerous obstacles being put in the way as the negotiations progressed. Finally, on 1 March 1644, a new treaty was signed in The Hague between King Louis XIV and the States of the United Provinces.

When the plenipotentiaries of the Queen Regent and of Mazarin arrived in Münster in July 1644, the international situation had become tense. Sweden had invaded Denmark without warning its French ally, and the French army had been defeated at Tuttlingen by the Imperials and the Bavarians (24 November 1643). Negotiations therefore began in an atmosphere of great suspicion between the Swedes and the French.

---

3   Bougeant, *Histoire des guerres et des négociations qui précédèrent le traité de Westphalie*, p.523.
4   Bougeant, *Histoire des guerres et des négociations qui précédèrent le traité de Westphalie*, p.526.

Within this framework, Mazarin's objectives were to sign an advantageous treaty and ensure its long-term execution. The task would prove long and difficult, however: while he wanted to weaken the House of Austria by retaining the positions it had acquired in Italy, The Netherlands, Germany, Lorraine and Roussillon, the latter naturally hoped that France would return its conquests to it.

1

The 1644 campaign

From 1643, although the Queen relied on him, Mazarin still had to reckon with the Princes who took a part in the Regency. According to the last will and testament of Louis XIII, Gaston d'Orléans, the King's brother, was *Lieutenant Général* of the State and the Army – he would in fact retain command of the Army of Flanders for himself – while the Prince de Condé was head of the Council. The chronicler Montglat[1] asserted that the Duc d'Orléans was a docile and well-meaning spirit, whereas the Prince de Condé, father of the victor of Rocroi, was a shrewd businessman who did not allow himself to be governed by anyone. Mazarin understood this. He was therefore going to spare the father, while giving his son, the Duc d'Enghien, the opportunity to acquire glory on the battlefield.

In Germany, the Swede Torstenson,[2] after wintering in Moravia, attacked the Danes, who were suspected of supporting the Imperialists.[3] *General* Matthias Gallas,[4] at the head of the Imperial Army, took advantage of the situation to retake positions in Bohemia, Moravia and Silesia. The King of Denmark called on Gallas for help, and Gallas moved towards Holstein to join his troops to those of the Danes. Warned of the threat, Torstenson returned to Germany and the two generals played cat-and-mouse with each other.

On 24 November 1643, at Tuttlingen, Josias Rantzau, *Lieutenant Général* of the Army of Germany following the death of *Maréchal* de Guébriant,[5] was

---

1 François de Paule de Clermont, *Mémoires de François de Paule de Clermont, Marquis de Monglat*, in Collection des Mémoires relatifs à l'Histoire de France (Paris: Petitot, 1825), tome 49, p.148.
2 Lennart Torstenson (1603–1651) was one of the best Swedish generals of his time. Nicknamed 'The Lightning Bolt' by his soldiers, he was particularly noted for his speed of action. Considered 'the father of field artillery,' he was also one of the best artillery generals of all time.
3 Queen Christina of Sweden wrote in her defence that Denmark 'has sought every opportunity to prevent the progress of our affairs in Germany' and 'has used every opportunity he could to embarrass us, so that he has forgotten nothing that could be prejudicial to us and our homeland.'
4 Matthias Gallas (1584–1647) was a general in the Imperial army between 1634 and 1638 and again between 1643 and 1647. He was better known for his faults than his qualities.
5 Jean-Baptiste Budes de Guébriant (1602–1643) was one of the best French generals of the Thirty Years' War. He was awarded the *maréchal*'s baton following his victories at Wolfenbüttel (1641) and Kempen (1642). He died on 24 November 1643 after having his arm blown off by a cannon shot.

THE BATTLE OF FRIBOURG 1644

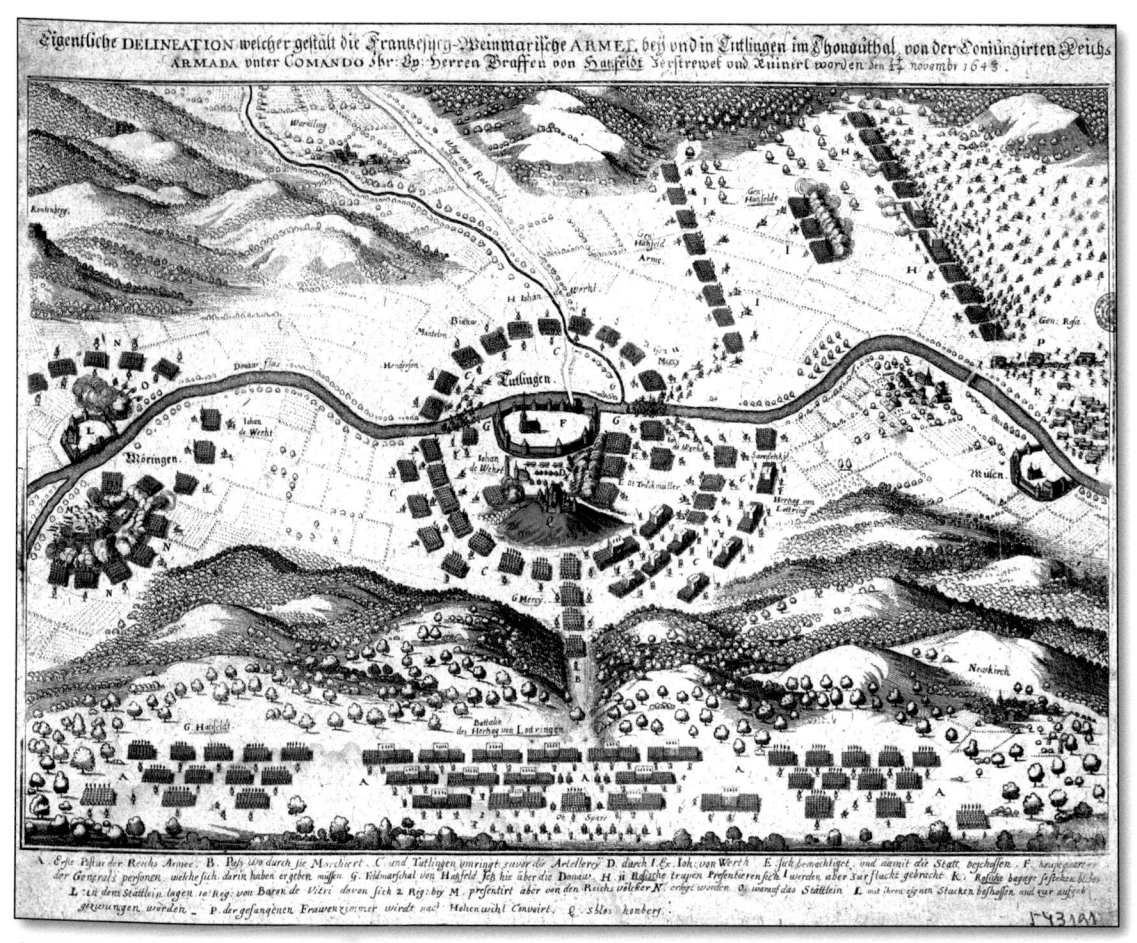

Battle of Tuttlingen, Matthäus Merian (BN Digital Portugal)

surprised by the Bavarian *Feldmarschall* Franz von Mercy. Rantzau and his three *Maréchals*, including Sirot, were taken prisoner and all the infantry of the corps were dispersed and scattered. The Regiments Guébriant, Kergroat, Castelnau-Mauvissière and Kolhass did not recover and were disbanded in early 1644.[6]

The command of what remained of this army was then entrusted to Turenne. He had earned his *Maréchal*'s baton on 16 November 1643 but had not yet been given a command and Mazarin was counting on him a great deal. On 3 December, he wrote to his plenipotentiaries who were negotiating peace in Münster that the Queen

> has resolved to spare neither money nor men to support the affairs of Germany and the Confederate cause. For this purpose, she has elected M. le Vicomte de Turenne, who is leaving at once to go to command the army, with good cavalry and infantry troops that he is leading, and plenty of money for food and generally for all necessary things.

---

6   Victor L. J. F. Belhomme, *Histoire de l'Infanterie en France* (Paris: Lavauzelle, 1893), tome 2, p.17.

And he adds:

> We are also going to make great and rapid levies, both in Germany and in France and elsewhere; to which I answer you, that money will not be spared. I am not talking about the qualities of M. de Turenne, who, in addition to the greatness of his birth, by which he belongs to the greatest houses of Germany, in addition to the character of *Maréchal de France* with which the Queen has recently honoured him, and his great capacity for the job, has worked for a long time in Germany and with the very people he is going to command, from whom we know that he is loved and esteemed as he deserves; and so we can promise ourselves that the reputation and advantages lost will be quickly regained under such a leader, and that the astonishment which might at first seize our allies on this subject will soon dissipate[7]

Mazarin then commissioned Turenne to reorganise the Weimarian army. According to Jules Roy, he 'knew Germany, he was known to the Weimarians; he had the calm, foresight and tenacity of Guébriant.'[8] While *Générals Major* Rosen[9] and Taupadel[10] were refitting the Weimarian regiments in this corps, the *Maréchal* arrived in Colmar in December. Erlach, Governor of Brisach,[11] still had to be spared his sensitivities. On hearing of Turenne's appointment, he threatened to leave French service – but the *Maréchal*'s and Mazarin's diplomacy changed his mind. During the winter of 1643–44, Turenne put all his energy into reorganising the army in Germany.

Johann Ludwig von Erlach, painter unknown (P. de Valière, Lausanne, 1940)

---

7   Jules Roy, *Turenne, Sa Vie, les Institutions Militaires de son Temps* (Paris: Hurtrel, 1884), p.53.
8   Roy, *Turenne, sa vie, les institutions militaires de son temps*, p.55.
9   Reinhold von Rosen (1604–1667), a soldier of Livonian origin, was one of the four directors general of the Army of Duke Bernard of Saxe-Weimar. In 1644, he was colonel of the 'Old Rosen' regiment and general major of the Weimarian troops in the service of France. His brother Jean was colonel of the 'Young Rosen' regiment.
10 Georges-Christophe von Taupadel (*c.*1600–1647), was colonel of a dragoon regiment under Duke Bernard of Saxe-Weimar. He has been colonel of a Weimarian cavalry regiment and *Lieutenant Général* of the Weimarian cavalry since 1640.
11 Jean Louis d'Erlach (1595–1650) was a Swiss general. He was colonel of a regiment in the service of the Swedes in 1625, general of the Swiss army in 1633 before entering the service of Bernard of Saxe-Weimar in 1635. He was appointed the French Governor of Brisach in 1638.

THE BATTLE OF FRIBOURG 1644

On 11 January 1644, Mercy laid siege to Überlingen. On 22 January, Turenne 'paid a watch to his army, which was growing larger by the day,'[12] and then, on 2 February, set up his headquarters in Remiremont. Throughout February, Erlach worked to raise an infantry regiment and a cavalry regiment to reinforce the army. At the beginning of March, while the Vicomte de Courval, Governor of Überlingen, was still resisting the Bavarians, Turenne visited Colmar, Brisach and Fribourg before returning to Lorraine. At the end of March, Mercy became impatient and went to the siege of Überlingen. A few French soldiers disguised as Bavarians had managed to supply the town.

Turenne's plan was set out in a letter to Mazarin dated 29 February:

> Your Eminence knows how the whole of the upper Rhine is held by the Swiss, and holding the lower Rhine in the same way, the whole of Alsace, the Palatinate on the Rhine, Lorraine and the county of Burgundy remain, with little work, as peaceful as the area around Paris. The Army of Germany would draw contributions from it, the country being a little recovered, and would have regulated quarters there, as the Army of Bavaria does in Württemberg; and in addition to that, we always have the entrance to Germany through two or three of the most beautiful places in the world. Even if at this time the country were returned to M. de Lorraine, he would be incapable of doing any harm, and the Rhine would serve as a boundary on one side, as the Somme does on the Picardy side, I mean up to the point where it joins the Moselle. I presuppose that Trier would also be taken, so that, on the German side, the only thing left to the enemies would be the electorate of Cologne. It can be said that we held Speyer, Worms and Mainz, and that we were unable to hold them. The reason is that we did not hold the upper Rhine, which will always ruin those who hold the lower Rhine, when we want to persist there, and that no bad event will happen there, for which we cannot respond. It is very certain that the strength of the enemies will make this plan difficult; but this is only to let Your Eminence know that, when daylight comes, this is not something to be neglected, since, remaining masters of these places, as soon as you are strong, you will be able to enter Germany, and being weak, at least you will prevent them from passing, and will be able to turn whatever forces you wish in Italy and Spain, having little to fear on the Rhine side, when you want, with a reasonable army, to put yourself on the defensive. With regard to the ease encountered in previous years, the enemies having always abandoned these places without any garrison, if we had some advantage this year, or that they could be drawn away from there, leaving Spire, Worms and Mayence deprived as usual, it would be necessary to make a small corps in Burgundy, when the armies would set out on campaign, which would join the garrisons of Alsace, and would perhaps have this effect with little resistance.[13]

---

12 Théophraste Renaudot, *Recueil des Gazettes et Nouvelles Ordinaires et Extraordinaires et autres relations des choses avenues toute l'année mille six cents quarante-quatre* (Paris: 1645), p.92.

13 M. A. Chéruel (ed.), *Lettres du Cardinal Mazarin pendant son ministère, recueillies et publiées par M.A. Chéruel* (Paris: M.A. Chéruel, 1872), vol. 1, pp.623–624.

Mazarin replied to Turenne that he would consider him carefully and make every effort to support him in his plans.[14]

At the beginning of April, Turenne captured Vesoul, Baume and Melzé in Franche-Comté. On 5 April, the *Maréchal* wrote to d'Erlach that he was leaving the three regiments of Schönbeck, Melun and Russwurm (Weimarian) in Vesoul and the regiment of Nettancourt with the artillery in Luxeuil.[15] On 15 April, he headed for the Lower Palatinate in the company of *Major Général* Rosen, returning to Remiremont on 5 May.

At the beginning of May, Duc Charles of Lorraine set out on a campaign against the French after signing a treaty with the King of Spain. His army was to cross the Meuse at Namur and march on the Moselle – Erlach was worried. On 11 May, after more than four months of siege, the Bavarians finally managed to take Überlingen.[16] Mercy then headed for Hohentwiel, but the place was strong and well defended. By 13 May, he was in Hüfflingen with his new objective being Fribourg. At the time, Fribourg was held by a Weimarian colonel, Friedrich Ludwig Canoffsky,[17] with his regiment and garrison of 1,400 infantry and 150 cavalry.

Cardinal Mazarin finally approved the plan submitted by Turenne, but preferred to entrust its implementation to the Duc d'Enghien.[18] On 16 May, Enghien swore an oath of loyalty to the King for the lieutenancy of the provinces of Champagne and Brie. The following day, he left to take command of the Army of Champagne. *Maréchal* de Guiche[19] was appointed *lieutenant général* to assist him. On 28 May, Enghien was in Verdun with his troops. A few days earlier, Turenne had taken the Army of Germany across the Rhine to observe the march of the Bavarians.

On 4 June Turenne's vanguard, composed of seven regiments of Weimarian cavalry under Rosen, fell on Mercy's vanguard commanded by Cosalky at Hüfflingen. Having taken 300 prisoners, he put to flight Truckmüller's cavalry regiment and three companies of Croats who made up this corps. Wolf's Bavarian dragoons, who had arrived as reinforcements, were quickly charged and routed. Gaspard de Mercy, Franz's brother, was taken prisoner but he managed to escape. On 8 June, following this affair, Turenne wrote:

> I returned yesterday from beyond the Rhine, where I thought I would have a greater effect. It succeeded quite happily, thank God, having taken seven cornets, a colonel, a major, three captains, many other officers and a thousand horses. We freed some of our prisoners and killed and took many others.[20]

---

14 Chéruel, *Lettres du Cardinal Mazarin pendant son ministère*, vol. 1, pp.623–624.
15 Albert d'Erlach, *Mémoires Historiques Concernant M. le Général d'Erlach, Gouverneur de Brisach* (Yverdon: 1784), vol. 3, pp.104–105.
16 Renaudot, *Recueil des Gazettes et Nouvelles Ordinaires et Extraordinaires et autres relations des choses avenues toute l'année mille six cents quarante-quatre*, p.387.
17 Kanofsky, in the German transcriptions
18 Roy, *Turenne, Sa Vie, les Institutions Militaires de son Temps*, p.58.
19 Antoine, Comte de Guiche, then Duc de Gramont (1604–1678), *Lieutenant Général* then *Maréchal de France* following the capture of Aire in 1641. He became Duc de Gramont on the death of his father after the capture of Philippsbourg in September 1644.
20 Philippe-Henri de Grimoard, *Collection des lettres et mémoires trouvés dans les porte-feuilles du Maréchal de Turenne, pour servir de preuves et d'éclaircissements à une partie de l'histoire de Louis*

THE BATTLE OF FRIBOURG 1644

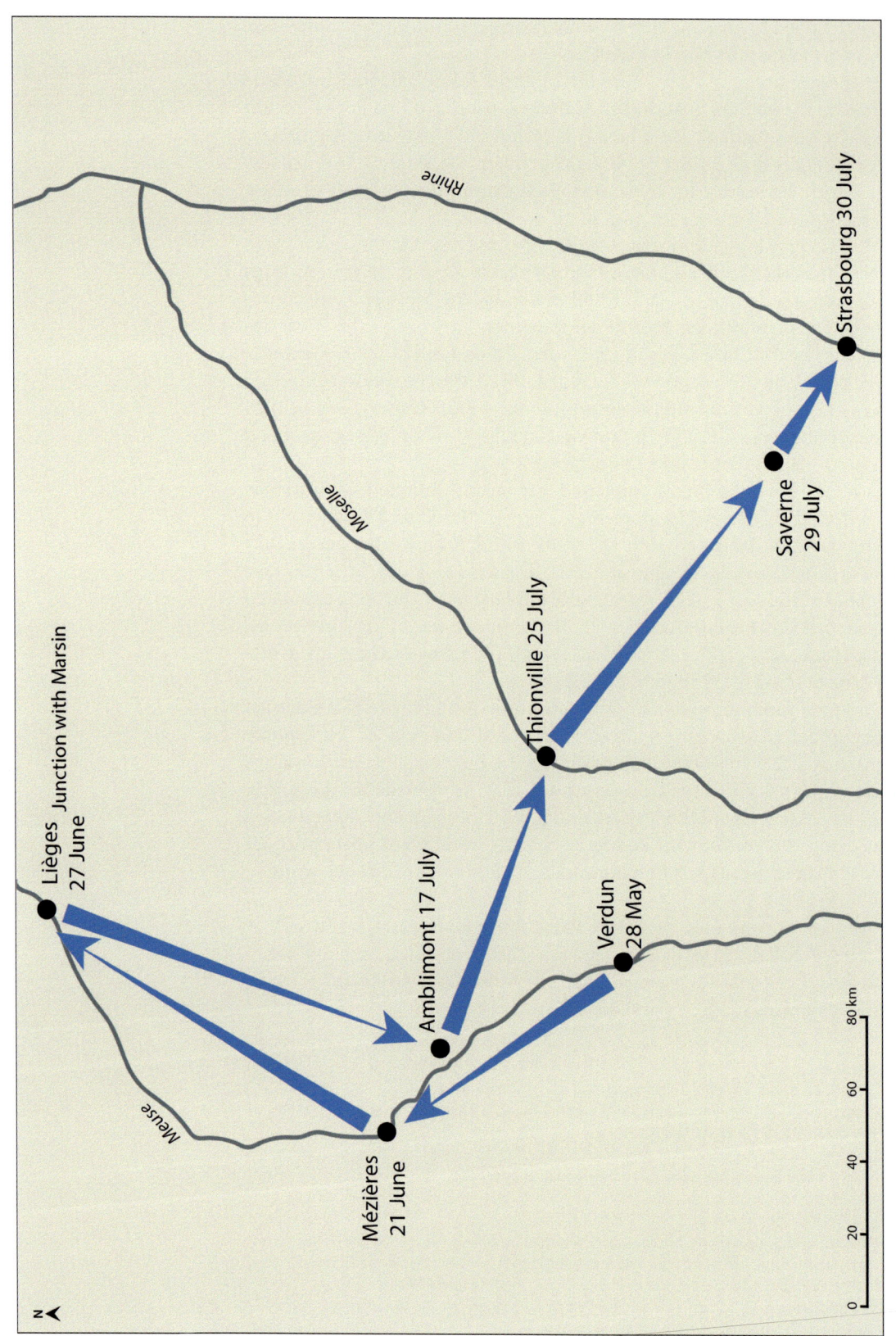

March of Enghien's army from 28 May to 30 July 1644.

On 21 June, Enghien was in Mézières. He had just received Mazarin's cavalry regiment of 600 *maîtres*,[21] which he judged to be 'admirably handsome',[22] and announced to the Cardinal that he now had 6,000 foot soldiers and just over 3,000 horse. He asked him to hasten and order the artillery horses to come straight to Mézières.[23] The young Duke then resolved to march on Luxembourg, to 'see if there was any way of doing something.'[24] He specified that he had no news of Turenne but that, if the latter could march on Trèves, or at least detach some troops to him, he could then lay siege to this place.

On Friday 24 June, Turenne sent Rosen, then the regiments of Melun and of Schönbeck with the artillery to Rheinfelden. The rest of his regiments followed. The next day he learned that the Bavarians were marching either on Fribourg, or on Laufenburg and the Basel region. At this time, the priority for the Queen and Mazarin was to stall to give the Duc d'Orléans time to take Gravelines. The town fell on 28 July after a two-month siege. The Duc d'Enghien was therefore instructed to observe the enemy and cover the border. Once Gravelines had been taken, the combined armies of Enghien and Turenne could then take places on the Rhine or the Moselle.[25]

On 27 June, Enghien joined forces with Marsin on the river Lesse in the Liège region. Marsin brought him reinforcements of 1,200 horse and 800 Liège infantry. On the same day, Mercy's vanguard appeared before the walls of Fribourg and Turenne wrote to Erlach about 'the enemy's attitude towards Fribourg.'[26] Turenne had no doubt that the town would soon be taken and asked Erlach to send him his troops. The same day, he recalled Rosen and Taupadel to him. On 3 July, Turenne asked the same d'Erlach to send him, 'one or two good guides who know the way around Fribourg, mainly on the Langen Denzlingen side, so that I can use them, should it be necessary to throw some aid into the said town from that side.'[27] He also stated that Jean de Werth[28] was marching on Brisach and that he had 'nothing certain about Fribourg, except that the enemies have not taken the suburb.'[29] Enghien was then at Cervisy, near Stenay. He wrote to Mazarin asking him to cover the Meuse, in accordance with his instructions.[30] On 4 July, Turenne asked Erlach to find out the position of four Imperial regiments of which he had no news.

XIV, et particulièrement à celle des campagnes du général français (Paris: Nyon, 1781), p.46.
21 Master: term used in the seventeenth century to designate a rider.
22 Henri d'Orléans, Duc d'Aumale, *Histoire des Princes de Condé pendant les XVIe et XVIIe siècles*) (Paris: Calmann Lévy, 1886), tome 4, p.577.
23 Duc d'Aumale, *Histoire des Princes de Condé pendant les XVIe et XVIIe siècles*, tome 4, p.577.
24 Duc d'Aumale, *Histoire des Princes de Condé pendant les XVIe et XVIIe siècles* tome 4, p.579.
25 C. Van Huffel (ed.), *Documents Inédits Concernant l'Histoire de France, et particulièrement l'Alsace et son gouvernement, tirés des manuscrits de la bibliothèque du roi, des archives du royaume et autres dépôts* (Paris: Charles Hingray, 1840), pp.10–11.
26 Albert d'Erlach, *Mémoires Historiques Concernant M. le Général d'Erlach, Gouverneur de Brisach*, (Yverdon: 1784), vol. 3, p.139.
27 Erlach, *Mémoires Historiques Concernant M. le Général d'Erlach, Gouverneur de Brisach*, vol.3, p.141.
28 Jean de Werth (1595–1652), cavalry general in the service of Spain and then of Bavaria.
29 Erlach, *Mémoires Historiques Concernant M. le Général d'Erlach, Gouverneur de Brisach*, vol. 3, p.142.
30 Duc d'Aumale, *Histoire des Princes de Condé pendant les XVIe et XVIIe siècles*, tome 4, vol. 4, p.581.

On 8 July, the Marquis d'Aumont carried out an offensive reconnaissance with 200 cavalry. The next day, Turenne had no news of the progress of the siege, but he thought that the Bavarians were waiting for the work to be completed, 'so as to be more certain of attacking it.'[31] On 10 July, Turenne learned from some prisoners 'that the enemies were not approaching the town at all: yesterday and today in the morning, they fired around 30 cannon shots to knock down a tower where they feared M. Canoffsky would put some cannon to harm them.'[32] The *Maréchal* presented himself before the besieged Fribourg but he found the enemy too well entrenched to attack. Mercy had an artillery battery set up on the mountain, a high point that allowed them to fire onto the town of Fribourg.

However, the French did not stand idly by: on 15 July, Général Major Rosen 'attacked six hundred Bavarian horses that had come out of their camp to surprise our foragers so severely that he took two hundred prisoners.'[33] On the same day, the governor of Fribourg told Turenne 'that he did not need any help and that he still had enough to make mincemeat of the Bavarians for a long time to come.'[34] The encampments of the French and Bavarian armies were close to each other, between Kirchhofen and Fribourg.

On 17 July, the Duc d'Enghien wrote to Mazarin that he was preparing to march on Trier in accordance with his instructions, but that he needed infantry reinforcements. Over the next two days, Enghien received two letters from Plessis-Besançon[35] informing him that Turenne was in sight of Fribourg, but that the Bavarian army was 'well posted' there. He concluded with: 'You must admit, *Monseigneur*, that it was a very bold move for *General* Mercy to commit to this siege so close to *Mr de* Turenne.'[36] The diplomat Plessis-Besançon also informed him that Duc Charles of Lorraine was on the march to join Beck's troops on the Meuse. He therefore asked him to temporarily suspend his march until he knew whether the Imperials had taken the initiative to cross the river.

The following day, 20 July, Enghien learned that the reinforcements he had requested would be with him on 10 August. Above all, Mazarin wanted Trier to be taken quickly so that he could then march on Luxembourg. On the same day, Turenne wrote to Mazarin that the Bavarians were 'ruining a lot of infantry' in the siege of Fribourg.[37] He suggested that Mazarin direct

---

31 Erlach, *Mémoires Historiques Concernant M. le Général d'Erlach, Gouverneur de Brisach*, vol.3, p.147.
32 Erlach, *Mémoires Historiques Concernant M. le Général d'Erlach, Gouverneur de Brisach*, vol.3, p.148.
33 Renaudot, *Recueil des Gazettes et Nouvelles Ordinaires et Extraordinaires et autres relations des choses avenues toute l'année mille six cents quarante-quatre*, p.596.
34 Renaudot, *Recueil des Gazettes et Nouvelles Ordinaires et Extraordinaires et autres relations des choses avenues toute l'année mille six cents quarante-quatre*, p.596.
35 Bernard du Plessis-Besançon (1600–1670), a marshal in the King's armies, was also a diplomat in the service of Richelieu and then Mazarin. From May 1644, he was in charge of negotiations with the Duke of Lorraine.
36 Duc d'Aumale, *Histoire des Princes de Condé pendant les XVIe et XVIIe siècles*, tome 4, vol. 4, p.597.
37 Duc d'Aumale, *Histoire des Princes de Condé pendant les XVIe et XVIIe siècles*), tome 4, vol. 4, p.597.

THE 1644 CAMPAIGN

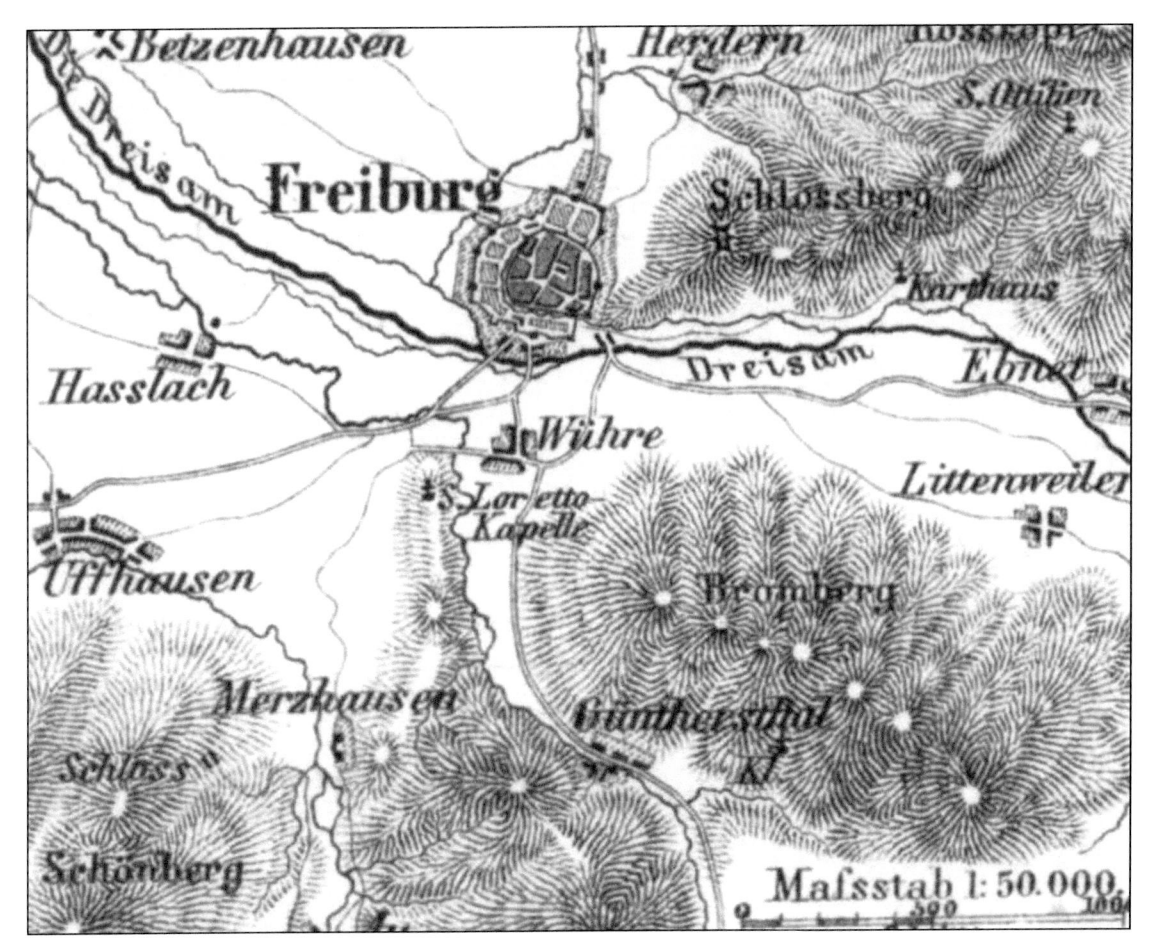

Map of Fribourg, 1880

the Army of Champagne towards the Rhine, as Gallas's army was engaged far from the river against Torstenson's Swedes. With Bavaria's army thus reduced, such a manoeuvre would enable him to take control of the Rhine as early as this year. He added that this army should be sent via Saverne and that if it was commanded by the Duc d'Enghien, he would obey him. If not, Turenne 'will contribute everything to come to terms with him.'[38] Finally, he wrote to d'Erlach that he was resolved to 'throw some people into Fribourg' and that he would like to know by what means this could be done most 'conveniently.'[39] A few days later, the *Maréchal* learned that the suburb of Fribourg had been taken.

On 22 July, the Duc d'Enghien informed Mazarin that, with no news from Plessis-Besançon and the Duke of Lorraine's march, he was continuing his own march towards Thionville where he would take steps to carry out the minister's plan. Four days later, when he was in Krozingen, a town a few leagues south-west of Fribourg, Turenne asked Enghien to advance towards Brisach via Saverne. He told him that he believed that 'there is no doubt that you will fight the enemy, as it is impossible for him to withdraw in the way he has undertaken below the mountains.' And to convince him, if need be, he added: 'if it pleases you to march diligently, I have no doubt that you will do the most glorious deed in the world.'[40]

On 27 July, Turenne wrote to d'Erlach to 'send a signal to Mr Canoffsky, of those you have agreed, when help arrives…. They have made an effort today against those inside, having heard a lot of shooting, which makes me fear that they will surrender before help arrives, which arriving in time, I do not see how the enemies can withdraw.'[41] The next day he reminded him to send signals to Canoffsky to warn him that 'help is not far off, so that he can hold out and defend for the time being.'[42] On 29 July, from Krozingen, he wrote to d'Erlach 'that it is to be believed that those in the town are treating' and he begged him to send signals to Canoffsky once again to ask him to hold out for two or three more days. He also informed him that Enghien was in Saverne and that he would ask him to hurry.[43]

But it was already too late. The surrender of Fribourg was signed on 28 July. On 29 July, Turenne announced the news to the Duc d'Enghien. Fearing that the news would stop him, he told him that 'having told them of our arrival, they will certainly drag on and give you time to arrive, and from all appearances we can only foresee the loss of their army.' Turenne added that he was pleasantly surprised that the Duc was already in Saverne and begged

---

38 Duc d'Aumale, *Histoire des Princes de Condé pendant les XVIe et XVIIe siècles*, tome 4, vol. 4, p.598.
39 Erlach, *Mémoires Historiques Concernant M. le Général d'Erlach, Gouverneur de Brisach*, vol. 3, p.150.
40 Duc d'Aumale, *Histoire des Princes de Condé pendant les XVIe et XVIIe siècles*, tome 4, vol. 4, p.602.
41 Erlach, *Mémoires Historiques Concernant M. le Général d'Erlach, Gouverneur de Brisach*, vol. 3, p.156.
42 Erlach, *Mémoires Historiques Concernant M. le Général d'Erlach, Gouverneur de Brisach*, p.159.
43 Erlach, *Mémoires Historiques Concernant M. le Général d'Erlach, Gouverneur de Brisach*, p.160.

him 'to continue, hoping that this journey will bring him much glory.'[44] In this way, the *Maréchal* hoped to make up for the loss of Fribourg. Why did Canoffsky surrender his arms, when he could not have been unaware that help was at hand? Was he approached by Mercy? The fact remains that neither Enghien nor Turenne would forgive him.

Ramsay states that on 28 July:

> the Court, informed that the King's army was too weak to attack the Imperials, ordered Louis de Bourbon, Duc d'Enguien to join the Vicomte de Turenne.

He goes on to say that

> against such an enemy [i.e. the Comte de Mercy], no less than Enghien or Turenne were needed: the Prince and the Vicomte were of different characters; but both animated by the same love of the public good, they always shared the same views, without anything being able to alter their union.[45]

---

44 Duc d'Aumale, *Histoire des Princes de Condé pendant les XVIe et XVIIe siècles*, vol. 4, p.602.
45 Andrew Michael Ramsay, *Histoire du Vicomte de Turenne, Maréchal-Général des Armées du Roy* (The Hague: Jean Neaulme, 1736), p.120.

THE BATTLE OF FRIBOURG 1644

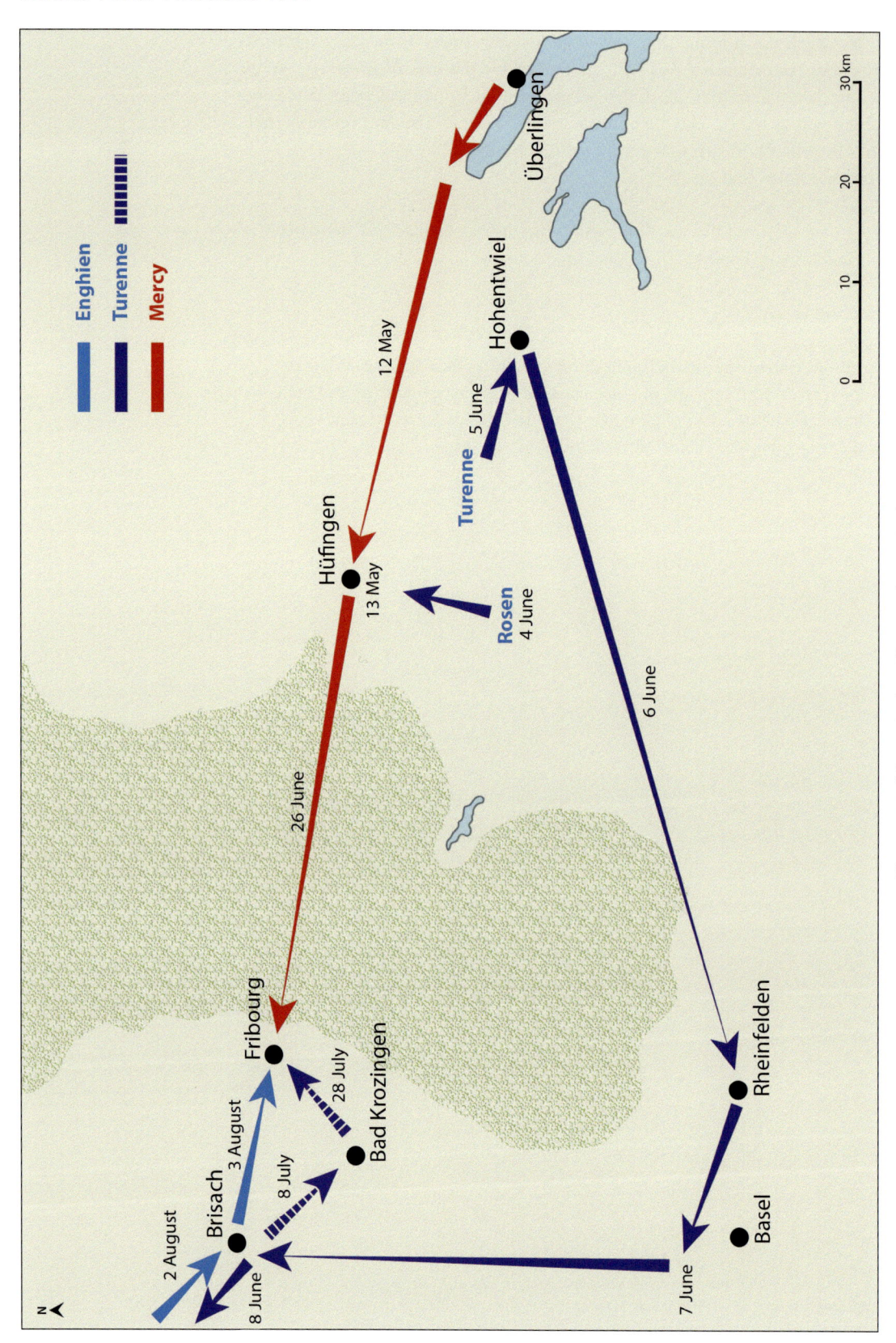

Movements of the armies from May 11 to August 3, 1644.

2

Commanders

The Duc d'Enghien

Born in Paris on 8 September 1621, Louis II de Bourbon, Duc d'Enghien, in 1644 was not yet Prince de Condé – he succeeded to the title on the death of his father Henri[1] on 26 December 1646. Educated for 6 years at the Jesuit college of Sainte-Marie de Bourges, he was presented to the King on 19 January 1636. At that time, the Prince de Condé had been given command of the royal army in Franche-Comté. The following year, the young Duc entered the royal academy for young nobility, located in Paris on the rue du Temple.[2] This academy, transformed by Louis XIII into a military school, taught its prestigious students mathematics, geography, cartography, fortification, fencing, horsemanship and good manners in addition to military exercises. In April 1638, having completed his studies, he was appointed head of the Burgundy government in the absence of his father, who had been appointed commander of the Army of Guyenne. Enghien was only 17 years old and the Prince made sure that no decision was taken without the advice of the council appointed by himself. Burgundy was a frontier region at the time, and war was on its doorstep.

Despite his youth, the Duc d'Enghien soon proved to be a competent governor and he ordered all the strongholds on the border to be inspected and repaired, and then checked the strength of the garrisons, the food supplies and the ammunition supply. These measures proved useful, as in May 1638, 17 cavalry squadrons and 200 enemy infantry set fire to the town of Selongey. Enghien had placed a company of riflemen in the vicinity and the enemy was finally repulsed.[3]

---

1 Henri II de Bourbon-Condé (1588–1646), Prince de Condé, first Prince of the Blood, he was Governor of Burgundy and Berry.
2 Duc d'Aumale, *Histoire des Princes de Condé pendant les XVIe et XVIIe siècles*, tome 3, p.335.
3 Duc d'Aumale, *Histoire des Princes de Condé pendant les XVIe et XVIIe siècles*, tome 4, p.349.

THE BATTLE OF FRIBOURG 1644

Louis II de Bourbon, Prince de Condé 1662, engraving by Robert Nanteuil (1623–1678). (Public Domain)

A few days later, on 23 May, Condé wrote to his son to give all possible assistance to 'his cousin the Vicomte de Turenne,'[4] who was then a *maréchal de camp* commanding a corps charged with opposing partisans from the Comtois and Lorraine. This was the first time the two men had been in contact. They exchanged a few letters. The Duc was already passionate about military affairs: he supervised troop exercises, reviewed them and manoeuvred them. Since 1635, he had been at the head of two infantry regiments, Enghien and Conti, a cavalry regiment, and four companies of *gendarmes* and *chevau-légers*. He made it a point of honour for his troops to set an example to the rest of the army: the companies had to be complete and disciplined.

In April 1640, Enghien was sent to the Army of Picardy, commanded by *Maréchal* de la Meilleraye.[5] That year, he took up arms for the first time as a volunteer at the siege of Arras, managing to take a captain of Imperial cuirassiers prisoner during an engagement.[6] He was only 19 at the time. In 1642, he was with the Royal Army in Roussillon. The following year, he was given command of the Army of Picardy, but the choice was a delicate one, 'was it appropriate to put an army in the hands of the House of Condé?'[7] He was nevertheless given the *Maréchal* de l'Hôpital, the King's *Lieutenant Général*, to moderate the ardour of his youth. Well advised, Enghien won his first prestigious victory on 19 May 1643 at Rocroi.

Although his exact role in this victory is still debated, the fact remains that the future *Grande Condé* was a courageous, charismatic and determined general. Naturally cheerful and playful, he proved to be an exceptional leader of men. Additionally, he already had the instinctive ability to make the right decisions. *Maréchal* de Gramont, who particularly admired him, exclaimed on the day of the Battle of Lens:

---

4   Duc d'Aumale, *Histoire des Princes de Condé pendant les XVIe et XVIIe siècles*, vol. 3, p.350.
5   Charles de la Porte, Duc de La Meilleraye (1602–1664), Marshal and Grand Master of the French Artillery, was the cousin of Cardinal de Richelieu.
6   Duc d'Aumale, *Histoire des Princes de Condé pendant les XVIe et XVIIe siècles*, vol. 3, p.435.
7   Duc d'Aumale, *Histoire des Princes de Condé pendant les XVIe et XVIIe siècles*, vol. 4, p.8.

His presence of mind and this perfect knowledge of men always put him above the others in the most perilous and the greatest occasions, because everything that had to be done presented itself to him in the moment. They are rare geniuses for war, and among a hundred thousand there is one of such a kind.[8]

Napoleon was more critical, reproaching him for his impetuosity, particularly at the Battle of Fribourg. And he also condemned the choice he made in 1645 to attack the Bavarian positions: 'The Prince de Condé was wrong to attack Mercy in his camp at Nördlingen, with an army composed almost entirely of cavalry and with so little artillery.' However, he agreed that 'Condé deserved the victory by that obstinacy, that rare intrepidity which distinguished him.'[9]

In 1644 Enghien was still young and feisty, however, constantly listening to his advisers, he learned quickly. Thus, capitalising on his past experience, he quickly became an excellent tactician. Five years after Rocroi, his victory at Lens, which remains one of his masterpieces, was the best example of this: on the day, he managed to lure the enemy army to the chosen ground and engage in battle at the right moment. He explained the manoeuvre to his officers, at the start of the engagement, by drawing a comparison with fencing: 'while the less learned beat their feet, without slackening their stride, the expert takes his time and lodges his boot to his heart's content.'[10]

Maréchal Turenne

Born on 11 September 1611 at the Château de Sedan, Henri de la Tour d'Auvergne, Vicomte de Turenne, began his military career in The Netherlands at the age of 14, under the orders of Stadtholder Frederik-Henri d'Orange-Nassau.[11] He had just enough time to get to know his uncle, Prince Maurice d'Orange-Nassau, before the latter died on 23 April 1625. Prince Maurice had demanded that the young Turenne 'carry a musket before raising him to any rank.'[12] In 1626, Prince Frédéric-Henri entrusted him with a company of infantry. The young Vicomte made it 'the finest and best disciplined company in the army,'[13] before taking part in the campaigns against Spinola[14] from 1627 to 1629. The following year, he entered the service of France, where he was received by the King and the Cardinal 'with all the distinctions that his

---

8   Antoine de Gramont, *Mémoires du Maréchal de Gramont*, in Nouvelle collection des mémoires pour servir à l'Histoire de France (Paris, 1839), troisième série, tome 7, p.280.
9   Napoléon Bonaparte, *Précis des guerres du Maréchal de Turenne*, https://gallica.bnf.fr/ark:/12148/bpt6k86480n.image, pp124–125.
10 Stéphane Thion, *French Armies of the Thirty Years' War, 1618–1648* (Warwick: Helion & Co., 2024), Century of the Soldier 1618–1721 Series no. 117.
11 Frédéric-Henri d'Orange-Nassau (1584–1647), Prince of Orange and Count of Nassau, brother of Maurice de Nassau, Stadtholder of several States of the United Provinces, was captain and *Admiraal Generaal* of the United Provinces.
12 Ramsay, *Histoire du Vicomte de Turenne, Maréchal-Général des Armées du Roy*, p.13.
13 Ramsay, *Histoire du Vicomte de Turenne, Maréchal-Général des Armées du Roy*, p.14.
14 Ambrogio Spinola (1569–1630), Marqués de los Balbases, was a Genoese soldier who served in the Spanish army during the Eighty Years' War and the Thirty Years' Wars. The painter Diego Velázquez immortalised him in the depiction of the surrender of Breda in 1625.

birth deserved.'[15] Indeed, Richelieu gave him an infantry regiment and the rank of *mestre de camp*.[16] He took part in the siege of La Mothe in 1634, after which, at the age of 23, he was appointed *maréchal de camp*. He participated in various campaigns between 1634 and 1639 – in Lorraine, on the Rhine, in Flanders, in Burgundy and in Picardy. His record of service and reputation earned him the opportunity to assist Henri de Lorraine-Harcourt[17] in Italy from 1639 to 1641. The following year, he was appointed *lieutenant général* to *Maréchal* de la Meilleraye, who commanded the Royal Army in Roussillon, and in 1643 he assisted Prince Thomas de Savoy at the head of the Army of Italy. Finally, on 19 December 1643, the Queen, grateful for his actions, 'sent him the baton of a *Maréchal de France*.'[18] Turenne was 32 years old at the time. At the beginning of 1644, he was sent to lead the army in Germany, which was in a delicate situation following the failure at Rottweil and the defeat at Tuttlingen. He put the army back on its feet, drawing heavily on his own financial resources.

Henri de La Tour d'Auvergne, Vicomte de Turenne. From an engraving of Nanteuil and a drawing of Pingebat, 1665 (Public Domain)

A great admirer of Alexander the Great, he was to become one of the finest generals of his time through his very qualities as a leader and strategist. He ensured that his troops were well trained and maintained, analysed conditions and the environment in detail, and was cautious before taking action but swift in execution once the decision had been made.

Napoleon approved of Turenne's manoeuvres after Fribourg, 'Turenne's conduct, after the departure of the Prince of Condé, was skilful; it is true that he was wonderfully supported by the local people. The armies of Bavaria and Lorraine were separated by the Rhine and the mountains; their junction was difficult.'[19] But Turenne's masterpiece probably remains his little-known 1646 campaign.[20] Napoleon himself admired Condé's manoeuvres against the Archduke, which he considered to be full of daring, wisdom and genius. In fact, he encouraged the military to study this campaign. When talking about the 1648 campaign, he couldn't resist returning to it:

> Turenne is the first French general to have planted the national colours on the banks of the Inn. In this campaign, and in that of 1646, he traversed Germany in all directions, with a mobility and boldness that contrast with the way war has

---

15 Ramsay, *Histoire du Vicomte de Turenne, Maréchal-Général des Armées du Roy*, p.21.
16 *Mestre de Camp*, or *Maître de Camp*, is the *ancien* name for the *Colonel* of a regiment.
17 Henri de Lorraine (1601–1666), Compte d'Harcourt, nicknamed 'Cadet the Pearl' after the pearl in his ear, was appointed Commander-in-Chief of the Army of Italy in 1639.
18 Ramsay, *Histoire du Vicomte de Turenne, Maréchal-Général des Armées du Roy*, p.107.
19 Napoléon Bonaparte, *Précis des guerres du Maréchal de Turenne*, p.119.
20 Just as is his 1674 campaign.

been waged since. This was due to his skill and the good war principles of this school...[21]

This outcome did not come about by chance. Like Bernhard of Saxe-Weimar, Turenne was able to bounce back from his failures, particularly that of Mergentheim (Marienthal) in 1645. Later, Ramsay would assert that he had inherited from his uncle Prince Hendrick van Orange-Nassau:

> the principles of choosing a camp well; of attacking a place according to the rules; of forming a plan from afar, rolling it around in his head for a long time, and making nothing of it apparent until the moment of execution; of being devoid of ostentation, and of filling himself with lively and elevated feelings for the interest of the Fatherland rather than for his own glory.[22]

From Bernhard of Saxe-Weimar,[23] he learned humility in success, the ability to rise again after failure, and the art of winning the love of his soldiers. From Cardinal de la Valette[24], he learned how to guard against court intrigues. Finally, from the Comte d'Harcourt, he learned that 'of all the military virtues, diligence and expedition are the most essential, and that they usually lead to success when they are accompanied by circumspection and prudence.'[25]

Feldmarschall Mercy

Franz von Mercy was born in Longwy in Lorraine around 1590 and he took up a career in arms at an early age, entering the service of the Elector of Bavaria in 1606. Mercy served with distinction during the first campaigns of the Thirty Years' War. In 1631, at the Battle of Breitenfeld, he was *oberstwachtmeister* under Piccolomini, probably within his cuirassier regiment (his brother Gaspar was captain of a company in this regiment). Piccolomini's Cuirassiers formed the elite of the Imperial cavalry at the time. It was an excellent school for Mercy, however, he was taken prisoner by the French shortly after the battle. In 1634, he served in the Black Forest, where he defended Rheinfelden against Bernhard of Saxe-Weimar. From 1635, the Duchy of Lorraine had been part of the Catholic League, fighting against France. The same year, Mercy was appointed *general wachtmeister* in the Bavarian army. In 1636 he was given command of the troops of the Duc de Lorraine, a corps under the Imperial *General* Matthias Gallas. Mercy was pitted against the army of the

---

21 Napoléon Bonaparte, *Précis des guerres du Maréchal de Turenne*, p.134.
22 Ramsay, *Histoire du Vicomte de Turenne, Maréchal-Général des Armées du Roy*, p.108.
23 Bernhard, Herzog von Saxe-Weimar (1604–1639), the eleventh son of John, Herzog von Saxe-Weimar, was one of Gustav II Adolph's best generals. In 1635, he entered the service of France.
24 Louis de Nogaret de la Valette d'Épernon (1593–1639), also known as 'Cardinal de la Valette,' was Archbishop of Toulouse and *Lieutenant Général* of the King's armies. He commanded the army in Germany with Bernhard, Herzog von Saxe-Weimar from July 1635.
25 Ramsay, *Histoire du Vicomte de Turenne, Maréchal-Général des Armées du Roy*, p.109.

THE BATTLE OF FRIBOURG 1644

Duc de Longueville.[26] On 15 August 1636, the Bavarian general entered Dôle alongside Duc Charles de Lorraine, but the rest of the campaign tarnished the general's image: his Croats burnt the town of Pontailler-sur-Saône, along with its inhabitants, and then destroyed several villages in the surrounding area. It took the heroic resistance of Saint-Jean-de-Losne at the end of 1636 for Mercy and Gallas to begin a difficult retreat. From 1638, Mercy led the army of the Elector of Bavaria. In 1641, he particularly distinguished himself against the first class Swedish general Baner.[27]

On 18 November 1643, Mercy succeeded in retaking Rothweil from *Maréchal* Guébriant, and this brilliant French general died of a wound received that day. A few days later, on 24 November, the armies of Mercy, Charles IV of Lorraine and Jean de Werth defeated Rantzau (who had replaced Guébriant in command of the French army) at Tuttlingen. As a result of this resounding success, Mercy was appointed *Generalissimo*[28] - General-in-Chief.

Mercy is rightly regarded as one of the most illustrious captains of his time. Gifted with a great sense of tactics, he shared with Enghien and Turenne a particular ability to make decisions and act quickly: his successes at Tuttlingen and Mergentheim and his exemplary behaviour at Fribourg are the best proof of this. Ramsay gave a perfect illustration of these qualities:

Franz von Mercy (Collezione Luca Cristini)

Among other eminent qualities, the Bavarian general had a superior ability to protect himself from surprise by the regularity of his movements; to penetrate the plans of his enemies as if he had been present at their councils; and to make up for the inequality of numbers by the choice of encampments. Against such an enemy, he needed no less than Enghien or Turenne.[29]

Mercy was also gifted with an excellent sense of organisation. As the Duc d'Aumale pointed out, under his command, the Bavarian army would become, 'the best of all the armies that sprang up in some way from the soil of Germany during this long period of war, not excluding the Weimarians.'[30]

Franz von Mercy was killed on the battlefield of Allerheim on 3 August 1645 by a musket ball to the head. The night after the battle, *Maréchal* Grammont lamented the sight of the remains of the man who 'commanded the Imperial armies with such authority, and who was so feared throughout Germany.'[31] His body lies beneath a stone in the Church of Our Lady in

---

26 Henri II d'Orléans (1595–1663), Duc de Longueville, Prince of France. He held several army commands between 1636 and 1641, in Franche-Comté, Piedmont, Alsace and the Palatinate.
27 Johan Baner (1596–1641) served under Gustav II Adolph between 1615 and 1632. He was appointed commander of the Swedish Army after the Nördlingen disaster in 1634.
28 Edward Cust, *Lives of the Warriors of the Thirty Years' War* (London: Murray, 1865), vol. 2, p.580.
29 Ramsay, *Histoire du Vicomte de Turenne, Maréchal-Général des Armées du Roy*, p.120.
30 Duc d'Aumale, *Histoire des Princes de Condé pendant les XVIe et XVIIe siècles*), vol. 4, p.448.
31 Gramont, *Mémoires du Maréchal de Gramont*, in Nouvelle collection des mémoires pour servir à l'Histoire de France, tome 7, p.263.

Ingolstadt. At the place where he fell on the battlefield of Allerheim, Enghien is said to have inscribed the epitaph *Sta, viator, heroem calcas* (Stop, traveller, you are walking on [the ashes] of a hero.)[32]

More than two centuries later, the then Duc d'Aumale paid him a fine tribute when he wrote that he:

> does not occupy the place in history that his character and merit assign to him. The man who led the attacks on Tüttlingen and Mergentheim, organised the resistance of Fribourg, withdrew his troops from the Saint-Peter defile, improvised the defence of Allerheim, combined the operations carried out by the Bavarians in 1643, 1644 and 1645, should have been included among the illustrious captains whose list Napoleon drew up.[33]

French halberdiers c. 1645, contemporary engraving by Jacques Callot. These figures may represent either officers or sergeants but are obviously a little more richly dressed than the rank and file, not least the centre figure who appears to have ostrich feathers in his hat – something beyond the purse of most ordinary soldiers. Similarly all three carry longer 'rapier-like' swords. The left and centre figures are probably wearing buff-coats but the right hand figure's 'antique' doublet, and short buff coat are oddly out of period, but everything else from Callot's work suggests he drew from life so it may be the actual appearance of this individual. (Stephen Ede-Borrett collection)

---

32   Cust, *Lives of the Warriors of the Thirty Years' War*, vol. 2, p.584.
33   Duc d'Aumale, *Histoire des Princes de Condé pendant les XVIe et XVIIe siècles*, vol. 4, pp.450–451.

3

The French Army in 1644

At the start of the 1644 campaign, the Royal Infantry consisted of 166 regiments, 31 of which were foreign. French regiments generally had 20 companies of 70 men (with the exception of the *Gardes Françaises*, whose 30 companies each had 200 men). Fifteen regiments had 30 companies, while 43 regiments had between 4 and 15 companies. The theoretical strength of 1,400 men for a 20 company regiment was almost never reached, and it was rare for battalions to have more than 800 men once the campaign had begun.[1]

The ordinance of 18 October 1643 on winter quarters therefore stipulates that regiments with fewer than 20 men per company must be dismissed at the end of the campaign.[2] As a result, the Regiments of Nangis, Souvigny, Ferron, Roqueservière, Clermont-Vertillac, Sivron, de l'Église, de la Mezangère, Gramont, Croissy and Thorigny all disappeared. The *vieux corps*[3] were to retain all of their companies, but for the others, only sufficiently strong companies would be maintained. The officers affected by these disbandments would be discharged, while the sergeants and soldiers would be incorporated into the old regiments or into the companies that had been retained.

Finally, during the winter, captains had to restore their company strength to 70 men, whether infantry or cavalry. Thus, the order of 20 December 1643 stipulates that the *Maîtres de Camp, Capitaines* and Officers must 'make their companies complete with seventy men each, armed for the infantry with two-thirds musketeers and one-third pikemen; and for the cavalry, each cavalryman with a pot,[4] a breastplate in front and behind, and two pistols.'[5] All the officers had to be present before the commencement of the 1644 campaign, i.e. by 15 February.

On 19 July 1644, Le Tellier wrote to Turenne that his infantry was 'weakened by the bad faith of the colonel and the avarice of the French

---

1 Victor L. J. F. Belhomme, *Histoire de l'Infanterie en France* (Paris: Lavauzelle, 1893), tome 2, p.19.
2 Belhomme, *Histoire de l'Infanterie en France*, tome 2, p.14.
3 The *vieux corps* referred to the six oldest French regiments, formed in the second half of the sixteenth century: Picardie, Piedmont, Champagne, Gardes Françaises, Navarre and Normandie, the last of which was formed in 1616.
4 A cavalry helmet, also known as a *capeline*, similar to the English 'lobster'.
5 SHAT archives SHD/SHAT A79-159

French infantry. Engraving by Jacques Callot, c. 1633. (authors collection)

officers.'[6] These abuses were commonplace, as shown by this extract from the royal order of 14 November 1643: *Pour la forme du payement des Gens de Guerre, & des Roolles à expédier pour la décharge des Trésoriers de l'Ordinaire & Extraordinaire de la Guerre,* renewing an order of 18 January 1641:

> His Majesty being well aware of the abuses that are committed in the matter of the watches and reviews of his troops, and of the payments that are made as a result, to the prejudice of his Orders and Regulations variously reiterated on this subject, even of the Order of the late King of happy memory, of 18 January 1641. His Majesty wishing to renew it, and in accordance with it.[7]

---

6   C. Van Huffel (ed.), *Documents Inédits Concernant l'Histoire de France, et particulièrement l'Alsace et son gouvernement, tirés des manuscrits de la bibliothèque du roi, des archives du royaume et autres dépôts* (Paris: Charles Hingray, 1840), p.17.
7   SHD/SHAT Series A A79-143.

THE BATTLE OF FRIBOURG 1644

French musketeer. (Lostelneau, *le Mareschal de Bataille*)

French pikeman. (Lostelneau, *le Mareschal de Bataille*)

THE FRENCH ARMY IN 1644

French musketeer. (Lostelneau, *le Mareschal de Bataille*)

Le Tellier added, in his letter to Turenne:

> I must confess to you in all honesty that it is quite difficult to fortify you with new corps, since the expenditure which we made during the winter to achieve this is so badly used; if you do not resolve, sir, to make some demonstration of severity against the officers, starting with those of your regiments, and that of your nephew, as having been the best treated, it will be even worse in the future.[8]

---

8   Van Huffel, *Documents Inédits Concernant l'Histoire de France, et particulièrement l'Alsace et son gouvernement, tirés des manuscrits de la bibliothèque du roi, des archives du royaume et autres dépôts*, p.17.

An infantry company consisted of a captain, a lieutenant, an ensign (or a second lieutenant), two sergeants armed with halberds, three corporals, three anspessadoes[9] and a drummer. The corporals and anspessadoes had the same weapons as the soldiers they command.

In theory, since January 1638, the cavalry had been formed into regiments of 8 companies of *chevau-légers* and a company of musketeers. In reality, regiments more often consisted of 5 or 6 companies of 70 men, rarely of 8 companies – reality and theory seldom went hand in hand. In 1639, for example, the Alais regiment had 11 companies, including one musketeer company; the Ferté-Imbaut and Gesvres regiments had 8 companies, including two musketeer companies; the Guiche and Brouilly regiments had 9 companies, including two musketeer companies; and the Cursol regiment had only 6 companies.

Gendarmerie companies were known as *franches,* meaning that they are not regimented.

The companies, with the exception of the gendarmes, consisted of 70 troopers who, at the beginning of 1644, were to be equipped with a pot, a cuirass and two pistols. This was, of course, a pious hope, regularly invoked by royal orders. The order of 14 July 1636 already insisted that 'horsemen should at least have a cuirass,'[10] an injunction that was to be reiterated in several orders, such as that of 27 March 1639, '[which] very expressly orders and enjoins all *mêstres de camp*, colonels and captains of cavalry, both French and foreign, to arm their horsemen with a cuirass in front and behind, a pot, two pistols and a sword.'[11] At the time it was the state that provided this equipment, as Sirot pointed out in 1642, 'The recruits were made in less than a month, and the cavalrymen were found in the numbers we wanted, so *Maréchal* de Guiche had me issue the weapons to arm them, which I distributed to all the regiments; but only enough were found to arm 2,000 horses, and there were still 1,000 unarmed.'[12] The gap between theory and practice is not anecdotal; for example, on 9 June 1639, of the eleven companies of *chevau-légers* in the *Colonel* regiment, four were armed,[13] one partially armed and six unarmed. Of the six companies of *chevau-légers* in the Gesvres regiment, two were unarmed. The Ferté-Imbaut regiment, had only one unarmed company of *chevau-légers* out of its six. The situation was

---

9   Anspessadoe or lancepessadoe: a term derived from the Italian *lancia spezzata*, meaning 'broken lance.' In France, this rank was created in January 1508: Louis XII instituted twelve places for lancepessadoes in the bands of Piedmont. These places were reserved for the nobility in order to attract them to the ranks of the infantry. This is how cadets from Gascony and ruined men-at-arms agreed to serve on foot.

10 Vicomte de Noailles, *Le Cardinal de la Valette, lieutenant général des armées du roi, 1635 à 1639* (Paris: Perrin et Cie, 1906), p.572.

11 Olivier de Varennes (ed.), *Vingt-troisiesme tome du Mercure François, ou suitte de l'histoire de nostre temps, sous le regne du Très-Chrestien Roy de France & de Navarre Louis XIII. Es Années 1639 & 1640* (Paris, 1646), p.43.

12 Claude de Letouf, *Mémoires et la vie de messire Claude de Letouf, chevalier baron de Sirot, lieutenant général des camps et armées du Roi* (Paris: Claude Barbin, 1683), pp.25–26.

13 In other words, the troopers were equipped with a pot and a breastplate.

THE FRENCH ARMY IN 1644

French *chevau-léger*, drawing by JOB (Jacques Onfroy de Bréville)

even more critical for the foreign regiments: the l'Eschelle and Fittingost regiments both had six companies, all unarmed.[14]

Neither of the two corps present in Fribourg included dragoons. However, Rosen had one regiment and Turenne asked Mazarin, at the very beginning of January 1644, to create a regiment of this type:

> M. Le Tellier has told me that M. de Tracy has been given a regiment of dragoons. I think it would be necessary to find someone in France to raise six companies. As Rosen's regiment consisted of six, there was one in each wing, and the four (other) companies remained with the supplies. It is very difficult to maintain dragoons.[15]

---

14 Du Bouchet, *Preuves de l'histoire de l'illustre maison de Coligny* (Paris: Jean du Puis, 1662), pp.984–985.
15 Chéruel, *Lettres du Cardinal Mazarin pendant son ministère*, vol. 1, pp.535–536.

Since Sully, artillery has included six models: the cannon with a 33-pound ball, which could fire up to 1,500 paces,[16] the large culverin firing a 16-pound ball, the bastard firing a 7½ pound ball, the medium firing a 2½ pound ball, the falcon firing a 1½ pound ball and the *fauconneau* firing a ¾ pound ball.[17] From 1635, French artillery benefited from the lessons learned from its Swedish allies, and the infantry used light guns of the *fauconneau* type in greater numbers. At Fribourg, the Army of Champagne had two demi-cannons and fifteen falconets, while the German army had six demi-cannons and fourteen falconets. The falconets were manoeuvrable and had the advantage of being able to advance at the same pace as the infantry, preceding it with destructive fire. Although this weapon was fragile, it could be manoeuvred by a single horse and had a range of 1,000 paces. From 1634, *Maréchal* de la Meilleraye was *Grand Maître de l'Artillerie* and the Marquis de Chouppes was his *lieutenant général* in the Army of Champagne. At the end of May 1644, Mazarin had 300 artillery horses sent to the Duc d'Enghien.[18]

Horseman 'capeline' and breastplate. (Museu Militar Marinha of Lisbon. Author's photo)

The Army of d'Enghien and Turenne at Fribourg

The composition of the French army presented in this section has mainly been reconstructed from the works of Ramsay,[19] Marichal,[20] de Serres,[21] and the Duc d'Aumale[22] and cross-checked with the works of Schaufler[23] and Guthrie.[24]

---

16   The pace is a unit of length dating back to the Romans. At the time, a step measured 2.5 feet, or around 75 centimetres.
17   Stéphane Thion, *French Armies of the Thirty Years' War, 1618–1648* (Warwick: Helion & Co., 2024), Century of the Soldier 1618-1721 Series no. 117.
18   Chéruel, *Lettres du Cardinal Mazarin pendant son ministère*, vol.1, p.717.
19   Ramsay, *Histoire du Vicomte de Turenne, Maréchal-Général des Armées du Roy*, pp.119–122.
20   Paul Marichal (ed.), *Mémoires du Maréchal de Turenne publiés pour la Société de l'Histoire de France d'après le manuscrit autographe appartenant à M. le Marquis de Talhouët-Roy* (Paris, 1909), pp.9–12.
21   Jean de Serres, *Suitte de l'inventaire de l'histoire de France* (Paris, 1688), vol.2, pp.951–956.
22   Duc d'Aumale, *Histoire des Princes de Condé pendant les XVIe et XVIIe siècles*, vol. 4, pp.577–608.
23   Hans-Helmut Schaufler, *Die Schlacht bei Freiburg im Breisgau 1644* (Freiburg: Verlag Rombach, 1980), pp.41–42.
24   William P. Guthrie, *The Later Thirty Years War; From the battle of Wittstock to the Treaty of Westphalia* (Westport, Connecticut: Greenwood Press, 2003), pp.202–203.

THE FRENCH ARMY IN 1644

Enghien, guide and *Mousquetaire du Roi*. (K. A. Wilke, Bibliothèque Universitaire de Lausanne. Photo by the author)

Ramsay states:

> the King's troops, of which the Duc d'Enghien was generalissimo, were divided into two corps: one called the *Armée de France*, made up of six thousand infantry and four thousand horse, under the command of *Maréchal* de Gramont; and the other called the *Armée Weimarienne*, commanded by the Vicomte de Turenne, made up of five thousand horse and five thousand foot soldiers.[25]

For his part, Paul Marichal quotes 6,000 infantry and 3,000 cavalry for the Duc d'Enghien's army and 4,000 to 5,000 infantry and 5,000 cavalry for Turenne's army, accompanied by 15 to 20 guns.[26] This first figure was confirmed by the Duc d'Enghien in a letter to Mazarin dated 18 June: 'I have six thousand foot soldiers and just over three thousand horse.'[27] De Chouppes gave a figure of 12,000 infantry and 10,000 cavalry for the two armies combined.[28]

---

25 Ramsay, *Histoire du Vicomte de Turenne, Maréchal-Général des Armées du Roy*, p.122.
26 Marichal, *Mémoires du Maréchal de Turenne*, pp 9 and 12.
27 Duc d'Aumale, *Histoire des Princes de Condé pendant les XVIe et XVIIe siècles*, vol. 4, pp.577–578.
28 Aymar de Chouppes, *Mémoires du Marquis de Chouppes, Lieutenant Général des Armées du Roi*, in Mémoires du Marquis de Chouppes, Lieutenant Général des armées du Roi suivis

THE BATTLE OF FRIBOURG 1644

French *gendarmes* and *chevau-légers*, watercolour by K. A. Wilke, (Bibliothèque Universitaire de Lausanne. Photo by the author)

THE FRENCH ARMY IN 1644

The Duc d'Enghien's troops formed the core of the Army of Champagne. They originally comprised the regiment d'Enghien, 20 companies raised in 1635, then the Conti regiment and the Persan regiment. To these were added the cavalry regiments: the regiment d'Enghien, four companies of *gendarmes* and a company of *chevau-légers* raised between 1634 and 1636. Other units were added to the Army of Champagne in 1643 and 1644: the Mazarin-Français and Mazarin-Italien infantry regiments,[29] the regiments Bussy, Le Havre, Fabert, Guiche and Desmarets (the latter from Liège); the Mazarin, Guiche, Beauveau and l'Eschelle cavalry regiments (the latter two from Liège).

The core of Turenne's Army of Germany was made up of the Weimarian troops of the late Bernhard of Saxe-Weimar, who had entered the service of France in 1635. At Fribourg, they comprised three infantry regiments (Hattstein, Bernhold and Schmidtberg[30]), not counting garrison units, and eleven cavalry regiments (Baden, Berg, Erlach, Fleckenstein, Kanoffsky, Alt-Rosen, Neu-Rosen, Russwurm, Sharfenstein, Taupadel and Wittgenstein). These German troops were joined by seven French infantry regiments (Aubeterre, Du Tot, la Couronne, Mazarin-Italien, Melun and Montausier) and three cavalry regiments (Guébriant, Tracy and Turenne). Since 28 December 1643, Schmitberg had been *général major* of infantry, replacing Schömberg who 'would not be in a fit state to come and exercise this office so soon.' On the same date, Schmitberg was authorised to raise an infantry regiment.[31] At the beginning of February, Mazarin gave the order to 'form a small corps in Alsace under the command of M. d'Erlach,' a corps that would depend on Turenne.[32]

---

des Mémoires Duc de Navailles et de la Valette pair et Maréchal de France et Gouverneur de Monseigneur le Duc de Chartres (Paris: J. Techener, 1861), p.69.

29 In addition to his cavalry regiment, Cardinal Mazarin raised several infantry regiments, two of which, Mazarin-Français and Mazarin-Italien, were present in Fribourg.

30 On 31 July, Turenne referred to the Schönbeck regiment *'which could make a brigade,'* but this regiment had probably been sent to Brisach. Erlach, *Mémoires Historiques Concernant M. le Général d'Erlach, Gouverneur de Brisach*, vol. 3, p.164.

31 Chéruel, *Lettres du Cardinal Mazarin pendant son ministère*, vol. 1, pp.520–521.

32 Chéruel, *Lettres du Cardinal Mazarin pendant son ministère*, vol. 1, p.579.

Table 1: The Duc d'Enghien's army in Champagne

Unit[33]	Type	Number of companies	Estimated strength
Enghien	Infantry	30 companies	800[34]
Persian	Infantry	30 companies	800
Conti	Infantry	30 companies	800
Mazarin	Infantry	30 companies	800
Le Havre[35]	Infantry	30 companies	800
Bussy-Lameth	Infantry	20 companies	800
Fabert[36]	Infantry	20 companies	400
Guiche (Liégeois*)	Infantry	20 companies	400
Desmarets (Liégeois*)	Infantry	10 companies	400
Total infantry (approx)			**6,000**
Enghien guards	Cavalry	1 company	200
Gendarmes d'Enghien	Cavalry	4 companies	600
Chevau-légers d'Enghien	Cavalry	1 company	150
The Queen's Gendarmes[37]	Cavalry	1 company	150
Enghien	Cavalry	6? companies	400
Mazarin	Cavalry	6? companies	600
Guiche	Cavalry	10 companies	600
L'Eschelle (Liégeois*)	Cavalry	?	600
Beauveau (Liégeois*)	Cavalry	?	600
Independent companies	Cavalry	?	?
Total cavalry (approx)			**4,000**
Artillery		4 cannons or demi-cannons & 15 falconets	

* Marsin's infantry and cavalry do not appear distinctly at Fribourg.[38] It seems that these men, 1,200 cavalry and 800 infantry, formed the L'Eschelle and Beauveau cavalry regiments and the Guiche and Desmarets infantry regiments. But there can be no certainty, as the *Gazette de France* lists the Guiche infantry regiment and the L'Eschelle and Beauveau cavalry regiments among those sent to meet Marsin in the Liège region.[39]

---

33 Renaudot, *Recueil des Gazettes et Nouvelles Ordinaires et Extraordinaires et autres relations des choses avenues toute l'année mille six cents quarante-quatre*, p.519.

34 Ramsay, *Histoire du Vicomte de Turenne, Maréchal-Général des Armées du Roy*, pp.124–125.

35 Chéruel, *Lettres du Cardinal Mazarin pendant son ministère, recueillies et publiées par M.A. Chéruel*, vol. 1, p.735.

36 Renaudot, *Recueil des Gazettes et Nouvelles Ordinaires et Extraordinaires et autres relations des choses avenues toute l'année mille six cents quarante-quatre*, p.519, gives Praroman's Swiss regiment.

37 Chéruel, *Lettres du Cardinal Mazarin pendant son ministère, recueillies et publiées par M.A. Chéruel*, vol. 1, p.746.

38 Chéruel, *Lettres du Cardinal Mazarin pendant son ministère, recueillies et publiées par M.A. Chéruel*, vol. 1, pp.510, 530, 610, 616, 617, 677, 713, 744, 756, 758, 760.

39 Renaudot, *Recueil des Gazettes et Nouvelles Ordinaires et Extraordinaires et autres relations des choses avenues toute l'année mille six cents quarante-quatre*, pp.518–521.

THE FRENCH ARMY IN 1644

Table 2: The Vicomte de Turenne's army in Germany:

Unit	Type	Number of companies	Estimated strength
Aubeterre	Infantry	20 companies	500
La Couronne	Infantry	20 companies	500
Mazarin-Italien	Infantry	12 companies	500
Montausier	Infantry	20 companies	500[40]
Melun	Infantry	20 companies	500
Du Tot	Infantry	20 companies	500
Schmidtberg[41] (Weimarian*)	Infantry	5–6 companies	500[42]
Hattstein (Weimarian*)	Infantry	5–6 companies	500
Schönbeck/Bernhold (Weimarian*)[43]	Infantry	5–6 companies	500
Total Infantry (approx)			**4,500–5,000**
Turenne	Cavalry		400
Guébriant	Cavalry		250
Tracy	Cavalry		300
Alt-Rosen (Weimarian)	Cavalry		400
Neu-Rosen (Weimarian)	Cavalry		350
Baden (Weimarian)	Cavalry		400
Berg (Weimarian)	Cavalry		350
Erlach (Weimarian)	Cavalry		400
Fleckenstein (Weimarian)	Cavalry		350
Kanoffsky (Weimarian)	Cavalry		350
Russwurm (Weimarian)	Cavalry		350
Scharfenstein (Weimarian)	Cavalry		350
Taupadel (Weimarian)	Cavalry		400
Witgentein (Weimarian)	Cavalry		350
Total cavalry (approx)			**5,000**
Artillery		6 demi-cannons (6-pdr) & 14 falconets (3-pdr)[44]	

* The remainder of the Weimarian infantry was in Brisach with d'Erlach.

---

40 Marichal, *Mémoires du Maréchal de Turenne*, p.10.
41 Chéruel, *Lettres du Cardinal Mazarin pendant son ministère,* tome 1, pp.520–521, 531, 536.
42 Erlach, *Mémoires Historiques Concernant M. le Général d'Erlach, Gouverneur de Brisach,* tome 3, p.164.
43 Several sources (Schaufler and Guthrie) list Schmidtberg, Hattstein and Bernhold as Weimarian regiments, but Heilmann writes that on 4 August only 3 officers and 50 men remained in the Hattstein, Schönbeck and Schmidtberg regiments. Johann Heilmann, *Kriegsgeschichte von Bayern, Franken, Pfalz und Schwaben von 1506 bis 1651* (München, 1868), p.672. On this, see also Erlach, *Mémoires Historiques Concernant M. le Général d'Erlach, Gouverneur de Brisach,* tome 3, pp.162 and 164.
44 Erlach, *Mémoires Historiques Concernant M. le Général d'Erlach, Gouverneur de Brisach,* vol.3, p.137; the French artillery had a total of 40 pieces according to de Chouppes, *Mémoires du Marquis de Chouppes, Lieutenant Général des Armées du Roi,* p.76; Johann Heilmann, *Die feldzüge der Bayern in den jahren 1643, 1644 und 1645 unter der befehlen des feldmarschalls Franz freiherr von Mercy* (Leipzig und Meissen, 1851), p.133, cites 37 pieces, 17 in the army of Enghien and 20 for Turenne.

One source (a version of Ramsay's *Histoire du Vicomte de Turenne*) cites the Mézières regiment in a brigade with the Montausier regiment. This regiment does not appear in any source and in fact never existed. On the other hand, when he joined up with Marsin in the Liège region, Enghien took with him '400 men commanded from the garrisons of Sedan, Mézières and Charleville,' hence the possible confusion.

The emergence of a new formation: the brigade

The first half of the seventeenth century marked a turning point in the development of infantry deployment. It was at the beginning of the century that the brigade appeared as a tactical formation.

During the sixteenth century, the infantry was grouped into large battalions of between 2,000 and 6,000 men, which took the form of squares; either of men i.e. with as many men in front as on each side (50 ranks of 50 files for a battalion of 2,500 men) or of ground, i.e. with the men occupying a square area of ground (150 by 150 feet, for example). Command remained relatively centralised and, despite the appearance in the French armies of *lanspessadoes* in 1508, and then of *caps d'escadres* – the forerunners of *caporaux* – under François I, army commanders did not take the risk of dividing these formations into more manoeuvrable autonomous units. It was not until Condé and Coligny that small independent formations of around 500 men appeared, notably at the Battle of Saint-Denis in 1567. Henri IV adopted this tactical vision when, in 1590, for the battle of Ivry, he aligned his infantry in small units of 500 men: each battalion of 500 Swiss pikemen or lansquenets was flanked by two battalions of 500 French arquebusiers. And the intra-army formations were taken even further – a cavalry squadron was inserted between each of these three-battalion formations.

Later, on the initiative of Maurice of Nassau, the Dutch War of Independence saw the use of small battalions of 400 to 600 men, but unlike those of Henri IV, Maurice of Nassau's battalions mixed pikemen and musketeers. The term *brigade* was not yet used, but the battalions were usually grouped in pairs. The deployment of the Prince of Orange's army at Juliers[45] in 1610 shows battalions grouped in pairs. The Danes imitated these arrangements fifteen years

French *chevau-léger* officer, watercolour by K. A. Wilke. (Bibliothèque Universitaire de Lausanne, photo by the author)

---

45 Juliers, or *Jülich* in German, is a town in North Rhine-Westphalia (Germany). The death of John William, Duke of Juliers, Cleves and Berg, in 1609 led to armed conflict. The War of the Juliers Succession ended in 1614 with the signing of the Treaty of Xanten.

later, deploying their army in 1625 on the same model: the battalions were grouped in pairs and placed in a diamond shape.

With the return of peace, the first 20 years of the seventeenth century saw the publication of military treatises based on the experiences of the French and Dutch wars of religion: *L'Art Militaire pour l'Infanterie* by Jean-Jacques Walhausen,[46] (published in 1615), *Les Principes de l'Art Militaire* by Jérémie de Billon[47] (written in 1608), and the '*Discours Militaires*' by Sieur du Praissac (published in 1614) are but a few examples. These three authors advocated the use of small battalions of less than 1,000 men lined up in a maximum of 10 ranks. For Billon, these battalions would be grouped in threes. Walhausen and Du Praissac show how a regiment, which remains the administrative unit, can be broken down into several battalions. But none of these authors used the term 'brigade'. This was not yet necessary, as in practice a regiment would be split into two or three battalions.[48]

This term was used by the Swedes and the French around 10 years later. Between 1617 and 1621, the Swedes organised their regiments into squadrons, a term equivalent to the French *bataillon*. Then, in 1627, Gustav II Adolph grouped these squadrons into brigades – a brigade being able to bring together squadrons from several regiments. These brigades brought together three squadrons between 1627 and 1628, then four squadrons, before returning to three between 1631 and 1634.[49] The size of these brigades was rapidly reduced, and by 1642 a brigade consisted of just one regiment, or 8 to 16 infantry companies.

Under Wallenstein's impetus, the Imperials were to follow suit, forming six *brigaden* in 1633, each comprising three or four regiments, i.e. 23 to 37 companies per brigade.[50] In this sense, Imperial practice differed from that of the Swedes because, as Montecuccoli later wrote: 'several squadrons and battalions were formed into corps or large members of the army known as brigades. Brigades are the vanguard, the corps and the rearguard, which march in front, in the middle and behind.'[51] However, following the example of Swedish practice, or out of necessity, the size of the Imperial brigades was to be reduced over time. By the time of the Second Battle of Breitenfeld in 1642, the Imperial infantry brigades numbered only 10 to 12 infantry companies, the equivalent of a regiment.

---

46   Johann Jacob von Walhausen (c. 1580–1627) was a German military writer. He planned to publish a compendium of military art in six parts, covering infantry, cavalry, artillery, tactics, fortifications and naval warfare, but he died before completing his work.
47   J. de Billon, Lord of Prugne. He joined the army in 1594. Three years later, Henri IV appointed him lieutenant of the Chappes regiment, which took the name of Nerestang in 1631. His *Principes de l'Art Militaire* was intended for all *young students of arms* in the Kingdom.
48   Thion, *French Armies of the Thirty Years' War, 1618–1648*, pp. 57–59.
49   Thion, *French Armies of the Thirty Years' War, 1618–1648* p. 119.
50   Otto Elster, *Die Piccolomini-Regimenter während des 30 Jährigen Krieges besonders das Kürassier-Regiment Alt-Piccolomini* (Wien: Verlag von Seidel & Sohn, 1903), p.48.
51   Raimondo Montecuccoli, *Mémoires de Montecuculi Generalissime des Troupes de l'Empereur, ou Principes de l'Art Militaire en Général* (Paris: Muzier, 1712), p.21. Raimondo, Conte di Montecuccoli (1609–1680) was born in Modena and was one of the great captains of the seventeenth century. He served as a general in the Imperial Army and was Turenne's opponent between 1673 and 1675. He also wrote *Memorie della Guerra*.

THE BATTLE OF FRIBOURG 1644

The French Army probably adopted the brigade a little before 1628. Merian Matthäus (1593–1650) left us a representation of the Royal Army in front of La Rochelle in that year: the infantry is formed into a diamond shape, with a group of two battalions at each vertex. This was the formation used by the Dutch in 1610 and by the Danes in 1625. In France, the term *brigade*, used to designate these groups of battalions, appeared by at least 1629. That year, at the siege of Privas, the regiments of Champagne and Piedmont formed a brigade.[52] At the Battle of Thionville in 1639, a brigade was made up of three battalions, two from the regiment of Navarre and the third from the regiment of Beauce.[53]. However, the idea of a brigade was not yet clear to everyone. The term *brigade* was used, notably by Louis XIII, to designate the two divisions formed in 1635 by *Maréchals* Châtillon and Brézé within the Army of Picardy. This was an excess of language used to describe the division of the army into two parts, which the King did not want. Each of these two *brigades* was made up of a large number of regiments and cavalry companies: 10 to 12 infantry regiments, each forming a battalion, and 26 cavalry companies forming 15 squadrons.[54] Each of the two 'brigades' was designated either by the name of the *Maréchal* commanding it or by the name of the *vieux corps* around which it had been formed.

The year 1644 is notable for the systematic use of infantry brigades within the French army. That year, the written sources list groups of two or three battalions formed for the Battle of Fribourg, even though our main sources do not explicitly use the term 'brigade': Espenan took the Enghien

Detail of the Plan of the Siege of La Rochelle in 1627, engraving by Merian Matthäus (BNF)

---

52 Thion, *French Armies of the Thirty Years' War, 1618–1648*, p.59.
53 Thion, *French Armies of the Thirty Years' War, 1618–1648*, p.101.
54 Stéphane Thion, *La bataille d'Avins, 20 mai 1635* (Auzielle, France: LRT Editions, 2011), pp.30–31.

and Persan regiments, Tournon the Conti and Mazarin-Français regiments[55] and Marsin the Le Havre and Bussy regiments. The Guiche, Desmarets and Fabert regiments probably formed a fourth brigade. In Turenne's army, the Weimarian regiments of Hattstein and Bernhold were supposed to form two brigades on 30 July,[56] but the following day Turenne changed his mind, writing that these two regiments were to form one brigade and Schönbeck a second.[57] The Tot and Aubeterre regiments probably also formed a brigade, as did the la Couronne and Montausier regiments and the Mazarin-Italien and Melun regiments. The *Veritable Inventory of French History* mentions six brigades for Turenne's corps: the Montausier & Melun, Mazarin, Turenne, Nettancourt, Schönbeck and Aubeterre brigades, but the Turenne and Nettancourt regiments were not present on that day.[58] Cavalry, however, did not yet use the brigade formation.

The brigade did not become a permanent formation until 1668, before that it was a temporary grouping. The ordinance of 27 March 1668 created the infantry brigadiers, whose role was to command the brigades.[59]

There was nothing prestigious about the French army that was to face its Bavarian adversary in Fribourg: there were no *old* infantry regiments, no *Gardes Française* and no *Gardes Suisse*. Most of the regiments, however, were permanent regiments which had already served in several campaigns. They were therefore units made up, at least in part, of veterans. The same applied to the cavalry regiments. Turenne's army was made up of the best in Germany: the Weimarian regiments of the late Bernhard of Saxe-Weimar.

In 1644, when he took over command of the army in Germany, Vicomte de Turenne had 5,000 cavalry 'reequipped and 4,000 infantrymen dressed at his own expense.'[60] He had to get this army, which had suffered greatly the previous year, back on its feet. At Mazarin's request, Turenne chose Aumont to command 'all the troops not covered by the Treaty of Brisach,'[61] in other words, his 'French' corps. Mazarin specified that 'he would nevertheless bear neither the title of *maréchal de camp* nor that of *lieutenant général*, but only that of commander of the French troops.'[62]

As we have seen, for the forthcoming campaign, his army would number 10,000 men, including 5,000 foot, 5,000 horse[63] and around 20 artillery pieces. The Duc d'Enghien's army would have a similar strength of around 10,000 men, including 6,000 foot, 4,000 horse[64] and 17 guns.

---

55 Ramsay, *Histoire du Vicomte de Turenne, Maréchal-Général des Armées du Roy*, p.256.
56 Erlach, *Mémoires Historiques Concernant M. le Général d'Erlach, Gouverneur de Brisach*, vol. 3, p.162.
57 Erlach, *Mémoires Historiques Concernant M. le Général d'Erlach, Gouverneur de Brisach*, vol. 3, p.164.
58 De Serres, *Suitte de l'inventaire de l'histoire de France*, vol.2, pp.953.
59 Belhomme, *Histoire de l'Infanterie en France*, tome 2, pp.136–137.
60 Ramsay, *Histoire du Vicomte de Turenne, Maréchal-Général des Armées du Roy*, p.115.
61 Chéruel, *Lettres du Cardinal Mazarin pendant son ministère, recueillies et publiées par M.A. Chéruel*, tome 1, p.660.
62 Chéruel, *Lettres du Cardinal Mazarin pendant son ministère, recueillies et publiées par M.A. Chéruel*, tome 1, p.660.
63 Ramsay, *Histoire du Vicomte de Turenne, Maréchal-Général des Armées du Roy*, p.122.
64 Ramsay, *Histoire du Vicomte de Turenne, Maréchal-Général des Armées du Roy*, p.122.

THE BATTLE OF FRIBOURG 1644

French Protestant officer and catholic foot, drawing by JOB (Jacques Onfroy de Bréville). (Author's collection)

The Duc d'Enghien's infantry comprised nine regiments – Persan, Enghien, Conti, Mazarin-Français, Le Havre, Bussy, Fabert, Guiche and Desmarets, the latter two from Liège – while Turenne's infantry included six French regiments – Montauzier, Melun, la Couronne, Mazarin-Italien, Aubeterre and du Tot, plus three regiments from Weimar – Hattstein, Bernhold and Schmidtberg.

The Duc d'Enghien's cavalry included his Gardes, the Enghien, Condé, Conti and Guiche *gendarmerie* companies, the Enghien, Guiche, Cardinal Mazarin, Mazarin-Français, L'Eschelle and Beauveau cavalry regiments (the latter two both from Liège) and companies of *chevau-légers franches*. Turenne's cavalry included the French regiments of Turenne, Guébriant and Tracy, as well as eleven regiments from Weimar – Alt-Rosen, Neu-Rosen, Fleckenstein, Berg, Baden, Wittgenstein, Russwurm, Scharfenstein, Erlach, Taupadel and Kanoffsky.[65]

---

65 Schaufler, *Die Schlacht bei Freiburg im Breisgau 1644*, pp.41–42 ; Guthrie, *The Later Thirty Years War; From the battle of Wittstock to the Treaty of Westphalia*, pp.202–203.

THE FRENCH ARMY IN 1644

The Marquis de Chouppes commanded the Duc d'Enghien's artillery as *Lieutenant Général*. Having taken up his duties, he began by ordering a review of the artillery officers and carriages. In mid-July, thanks to Mazarin's support against the Duc d'Enghien, he obtained precedence for artillery commanders over *sergents de battaille*. At the time, the artillery of the combined armies consisted of almost 40 artillery pieces, well supplied with various types of ammunition.

Within the Army of Champagne, were *Maréchals de Camp* d'Espenan, the Comte de Tournon and Palluau.[66] *Maréchal* de Castelnau-Mauvissière and Mauvilliers (or Mauvilly), and *Lieutenant de chevau-légers* d'Enghien, were *Maréchals de Bataille*.[67]

Artillery, engraving by Stefano Della Bella, from Thomas Dodd, *A Collection of Etchings by that Inimitable Artist Stefano Della Bella* (London: H.R. Young, 1818). (Public Domain)

---

66 The *Maréchals* organised the army's camp and accommodation, in consultation with the army general. During battle, the *Maréchals* commanded one of the army's corps (one of the wings or the reserve).

67 The position of *Maréchal de Bataille* was created at the end of the reign of Louis XIII (around 1643). The officer's main function was to place the army in order of battle according to the decided plan. In practice, he was assisted by *sergents de battaille*.

4

The Bavarian army

From the start of the Thirty Years' War, the Bavarians formed the core of the Catholic League's armies.[1] When Tilly died in the spring of 1632, the Bavarian units were absorbed into the Imperial Army of Wallenstein and his successors. After the Battle of Nördlingen in 1634, a predominantly Bavarian army gradually reappeared, such as Götz's corps, which fought at Rheinfelden in 1638. That year, Mercy took command of an exclusively Bavarian army.

The Bavarian Army had 21 infantry regiments and 30 cavalry regiments during the Thirty Years' War.[2] The Army's organisation was comparable to that of the Imperial Army. In theory, the Bavarian infantry was organised into regiments of 10 companies of 300 men each plus officers at regimental level. However, the commissions were not always respected, and in practice the regiments consisted of 8 to 13 companies of theoretically 200 to 300 men.

With ten companies, an infantry regiment could therefore muster, on paper, between 1,500 and 4,000 men, whereas a cavalry regiment could have between 500 and 1,000 men. In practice, of course, this was never the case. In 1638, Götz's infantry companies numbered between 45 and 150 men, with an average of around 100. Similarly, in 1642, Mercy's army's infantry companies numbered between 70 and 120 men.

The ranks of an infantry company were particularly well-filled and complete, with enlisted men accounting for less than two-thirds of the strength. For example, on 3 June 1644, a company of the Wahl regiment garrisoned in Ingolstadt included: a *hauptmann* (captain), a *lieutenant*, a *fähnrich* (ensign), a *feldwaibel* (sergeant), a reformado *feldwaibel*, a *lehrer* (tutor), a *furier* (armourer), a *musterchreiber* (secretary), a *feldscherer* (barber), 6 *corporäle* (corporals), 3 *trommelschläger* (drummers), 5 *leib und fourierschützen* (quartermasters armourer), 13 *gefreite* (first class soldiers) and 64 soldiers, making a total of 100 men.[3] In addition to these numbers, the

---

[1] The Catholic League or Holy Catholic League is a military alliance of the Catholic German states. It was founded in 1609 by Duke Maximilian of Bavaria.
[2] Laurence Spring, *The Bavarian Army during the Thirty Years' War – 1618-1648* (Helion & Company Limited, 2017), Century of the Soldier 1618–1721 no.15, p.41.
[3] Johann Heilmann, *Kriegsgefchichte von Bayern, Franken, Pfalz und Schwaben von 1506 bis 1651* (München: Literarisch-Artistische, 1868), p.897.

regiment's command and staff (Colonel, Provost Marshal, Quartermaster, Chaplain, et cetera) have to be added.

The division between pikemen and musketeers was comparable to that in the Imperial armies, i.e. one-third pikes to two-thirds muskets. Raimondo Montecuccoli, Turenne's future great adversary, stated, 'the [Imperial] infantry regiments are composed of two-thirds musketeers and one-third pikemen.' He added 'arquebuses are no longer used in German troops, because muskets carry further, and the man who would carry an arquebus can carry a musket.'[4]

In the 1640s, Montecuccoli proposed that the Imperial infantry battalions should be composed of 500, 1000 and 1500 men 6 ranks deep. He then proposed forming battalions with a central body of 480 pikes, '6 deep and 80 abreast, in front of which is a rank of 80 musketeers, who are covered by the pikes and can fire safely either standing or on one knee…. In front of this rank of musketeers is a rank of 80 targeteers [*rondaches*], covering everything behind.'[5] The pikes were supported on the flanks by two groups of 400 musketeers (10 squads of 40 men), one each side, some of whom could be alternately placed behind the pikemen and others 'posted between the nearest cavalry, from where they fired continuously until the melee began, at which point they withdrew to the battalions from which they had been drawn.'[6] Montecuccoli's ideal battalion

Early Bavarian infantry, watercolour by K. A. Wilke. (Bibliothèque Universitaire de Lausanne, author's photo)

---

4   Raimondo Montecuccoli, *Mémoires de Montecuculi Generalissime des Troupes de l'Empereur, ou Principes de l'Art Militaire en Général* (Paris: Muzier, 1712), p.29.
5   Montecuccoli, *Mémoires de Montecuculi Generalissime des Troupes de l'Empereur, ou Principes de l'Art Militaire en Général*, p.47.
6   Montecuccoli, *Mémoires de Montecuculi Generalissime des Troupes de l'Empereur, ou Principes de l'Art Militaire en Général*, p.48.

THE BATTLE OF FRIBOURG 1644

therefore comprised 1,440 men, divided into 480 pikemen, 880 musketeers and 80 targeteers.

The pike was considered to be the Queen of infantry weapons. Neither the pike nor the musket had changed since the beginning of the century. Montecuccoli says:

> Arquebuses are no longer used in German troops because the musket carries further, and the man who would carry an arquebus can carry a musket. Musketeers must carry a forked rest to better adjust their shot. [As for pikes, they] must be strong, straight and fifteen, sixteen and seventeen feet long [4½ to 5 metres], with carp's tongue points. The pikemen must be armed with helmets and have breastplates that cover them front and back.... The musketry alone, without pikemen, cannot form a corps capable of withstanding the impetuosity of the cavalry that surrounds it, nor the shock and encounter of the pikemen; thus they are obliged to give way.[7]

Bavarian musketeer, watercolour by Boisselier. (Public domain)

The Bavarian cavalry was formed into regiments of 5 to 10 companies each of 100 men. Out of the 13 cavalry regiments, a list dated 21 January 1639 shows four regiments with 10 companies (Behlen, Götz, Wahl and Wartenberg), one regiment with 9 companies (Kolb), four regiments with 6 companies (Harthausen, Redetti, Ruischenberg and Truckmüller), one regiment with 5 companies (Meissinger), one regiment with 2 companies (Lohn) and one company of Croats. On 19 November 1640, a further record showed four 9 company cavalry regiments (Gayling, Lowenstein, Werth and Truckmüller), four 8 company regiments (Kolb, Reuneck, Sport and Wert), a 6 company regiment (Wolf) and a 5 company regiment (Ossena), the last two regiments were dragoons.[8]

The actual strength of cavalry companies was generally closer to their theoretical establishment than for infantry. The establishment was 90 men in 1640 and 93 or 100 men at various times in 1642. But it could, of course, be lower, as in the case of the Kolb regiment in 1648, which averaged only 80 men per company.

---

7   Montecuccoli, *Mémoires de Montecuculi Generalissime des Troupes de l'Empereur, ou Principes de l'Art Militaire en Général*, p.30.
8   Heilmann, *Kriegsgefchichte von Bayern, Franken, Pfalz und Schwaben von 1506 bis 1651*, p.924.

THE BAVARIAN ARMY

The Bavarian cavalry, similar to its Imperial counterpart, retained the distinction between cuirassiers and mounted harquebusiers. In addition to these two arms, the more versatile dragoons and several regiments of 'Croats' formed the light cavalry. Four regiments of cuirassiers, three of mounted arquebusiers and two of dragoons were thus drawn up at Fribourg.

Montecuccoli described the cuirassiers of the late 1640s as:

> armed today with half armour, which has a front and a back, with burgonets consisting of several iron plates attached together at the back and at the sides to cover the collar and the ears, and with gauntlets, which cover the hand up to the elbow. The fronts of the cuirass must be musket-proof, and the other parts pistol-proof and sword-proof. Their offensive weapons are the pistol and a long sword that strikes with a thrust. The front rank could have muskets …. Full breastplates are admirable for breaking and supporting; but having recognised that if these weapons are not proofed, they are of little use, and that even, if the iron breaks, the pieces make the wound worse; and that, on the contrary, if they are tried and proofed, they are too heavy and embarrass the person so much that, once the horse has fallen, the rider is unable to help himself; that, moreover, armbands

German Kürassier in full armour, watercolour by K. A. Wilke. (Bibliothèque Universitaire de Lausanne, author's photograph)

49

THE BATTLE OF FRIBOURG 1644

and shorts break saddles and harnesses, injure horses on the back and tire them a great deal, it was deemed appropriate to stick to half armour.[9]

The mounted arquebusiers were theoretically less well protected, but added the harquebus to their armament:

Mounted harquebusier in breastplate, watercolour by K. A. Wilke (Bibliothèque Universitaire de Lausanne, author's photo)

> The harquebusiers or carabiniers cannot form a solid body, nor can they wait firmly for the enemy's shock, because they have no defensive weapons: this is why it would not be advisable to have a large number of them in battle, because they cannot be placed unless they cause confusion by turning their backs. As their job is to turn and caracole, to discharge and then to withdraw if the enemy presses them from behind, and they withdraw so quickly that it looks like flight, they take away the courage of the others, or they collide with them and fall on top of them. This is what determined Wallenstein, General of the Emperor's troops, to ban them from the army after the disastrous experience he had at the battle of Lützen in 1632.[10]

In practice, depending on their actual equipment, cuirassiers and arquebusiers were not necessarily distinguishable. In addition, the companies of some cavalry regiments had different compositions. For example, in August 1645, *Obristleutnant* Graf Boussu, in charge of the Imperial Piccolomini Regiment, ordered 200 'cuirasses' (i.e. two companies of cuirassiers) and 300 'carbines' (i.e. 3 companies of mounted harquebusiers) for his regiment, which numbered 500 men.[11]

It was not until the 1640s, therefore, that the Bavarian cuirassiers began to become lighter, like the Swedes or the French, and were equipped as described above. Previously, Wallenstein does not appear to have authorised this development, as Montecuccoli implies when he refers to Wallenstein's decision after the battle of Lützen. In January

---

9 Montecuccoli, *Mémoires de Montecuculi Generalissime des Troupes de l'Empereur, ou Principes de l'Art Militaire en Général*, pp.32–33.
10 Montecuccoli, *Mémoires de Montecuculi Generalissime des Troupes de l'Empereur, ou Principes de l'Art Militaire enGgénéral*, pp.32–33.
11 Elster, *Die Piccolomini-Regimenter während des 30jährigen Krieges besonders das Kürassier-Regiment Alt-Piccolomini*, p.94.

1645, Piccolomini asked to abandon full armour, at least for his regiment. Lieutenant colonel Graff wrote that 'the heavy and cumbersome full cuirasses, which distinguish cuirassiers from harquebusiers,' should be replaced by a helmet and a two-part, bulletproof cuirass. He argued that, when it froze, the men complained about the *brazallen* (armour with an iron glove) which 'could not be worn and could break.' Lastly, he specified that, as Piccolomini had wished, 'we will put in place 20 *carabins* per company, who will be most effective.'[12] This is the Imperial cavalry regiment of the 1640s and 1650s, as described by Montecuccoli above.

Artillery pieces, watercolour by K. A. Wilke. (Bibliothèque Universitaire de Lausanne, photo by the author)

---

12 Elster, *Die Piccolomini-Regimenter während des 30 Jährigen Krieges besonders das Kürassier-Regiment Alt-Piccolomini*, p.90.

Finally, according to Montecuccoli, the role of the Imperial dragoon was little different from that of its Swedish counterpart:

> they are nothing more than mounted infantry armed with light muskets, a little shorter than the others, half-pikes and swords, to seize a post in a hurry, and to warn the enemy in a passage. To do this, they are given hoes and spades. They are placed on horseback in the middle of battalion gaps to fire from there over the others; moreover, they usually fight on foot.[13]

Each company of Bavarian dragoons normally consisted of a *hauptmann* (captain), a *lieutenant* (lieutenant), a *fähnriche* (guidon) and a *wachtmeister*, a rank corresponding to that of sergeant, for around a hundred men.[14]

Finally, the Bavarian army was of course accompanied by artillery. In Fribourg, this artillery consisted of 24-pdr *halbe kartaunen* (demi-cannon), 12-pdr *schlangen* (serpentines), 5-pdr *falkonen* (falcons), 3-pound *falkonets* (falconets) and *mörsers* (mortars). A gun such as a falconet was manned by a gunner, four pioneers and a carriage pulled by one or more horses. 16 horses were needed per gun for a demi-cannon, 12 to 14 for a demi-culverin, 6 to 8 for a falcon or mortar and 4 to 6 for a falconet.[15]

The Bavarian Army under Mercy at Fribourg

To look at Mercy's army at Fribourg, I have relied primarily on the works of Johann Heilmann, *Kriegsgefchichte von Bayern, Franken, Pfalz und Schwaben von 1506 bis 1651*, Hans-Helmut Schaufler, *Die Schlacht bei Freiburg im Breisgau 1644*, and William P. Guthrie, *The Later Thirty Years' War*, bearing in mind that the latter two draw on the former.

Ramsay states that 'the Bavarian Army [of *Feldmarschall*[16] von Mercy] numbered around fifteen thousand men.'[17] Heilmann quoted around 20,000 men and 28 artillery pieces on 18 July, excluding artillery – 9,927 infantry under Ruischenberg and 9,713 cavalry under Jean de Werth. The infantry comprised eleven regiments, Wahl, Mercy, Ruischenberg, Hasslang, Gold, Holz, Winterscheid, Miehr, Rouyer, Fugger and Entschering, with a total of 94 companies,[18]

On 18 July 1644, the cavalry included four regiments of cuirassiers (Mercy, Gayling, Kolb and Lapierre), three regiments of mounted harquebusiers (de Werth, Sporck and Cosalky) and two regiments of dragoons (Wolf and Kurnreuter).[19]

---

13 Montecuccoli, *Mémoires de Montecuculi Generalissime des Troupes de l'Empereur, ou Principes de l'Art Militaire en Général*, p.32.
14 Heilmann, *Kriegsgefchichte von Bayern, Franken, Pfalz und Schwaben von 1506 bis 1651*, p.922.
15 Heilmann, *Kriegsgefchichte von Bayern, Franken, Pfalz und Schwaben von 1506 bis 1651*, pp.952–955.
16 Rank equivalent to a French *Maréchal*.
17 Ramsay, *Histoire du Vicomte de Turenne, Maréchal-Général des Armées du Roy*, p.122.
18 Heilmann, *Kriegsgefchichte von Bayern, Franken, Pfalz und Schwaben von 1506 bis 1651*, p.897.
19 Heilmann, *Kriegsgefchichte von Bayern, Franken, Pfalz und Schwaben von 1506 bis 1651*, p.925.

THE BAVARIAN ARMY

Table 3, Mercy's Bavarian army according to Heilmann

Unit	Type	# companies	Strength (18 July 1644)
Wahl	Infantry	6	705
Mercy	Infantry	10	1,031
Ruischenberg	Infantry	11	971
Hasslang	Infantry	8	741
Gold	Infantry	8	1,064
Holz	Infantry	8	977
Winterscheid	Infantry	8	951
Miehr	Infantry	9	850
Rouyer	Infantry	8	862
Fugger	Infantry	8	900
Enschering	Infantry	10	929
Sub Total, 18 July			**9,981**
Sub Total, at Fribourg			**8,000**
Mercy (Kur.)	Cavalry	8	800
Gayling (Kur.)	Cavalry	9	900
Kolb (Kur.)	Cavalry	8	800
Lapierre (Kur.)	Cavalry	9	900
Werth (Ark.)	Cavalry	8	800
Sporck (Ark.)	Cavalry	10	1,000
Cosalky (Ark.)	Cavalry	8	800[20]
Wolf	Dragoons	6	600
Kurnreuter?	Dragoons	?	600
Sub Total, 18 July			**7,200**
Sub Total, at Fribourg			**7,000**

Artillery: 4 demi-cannon (24-lb), 5 demi-culverins (12-lb), 8 falcons (4-lb), 3 falconets (3-lb), 3 mortars.[21]

Jean de Werth commanded the Bavarian cavalry, assisted by *Feldmarschall* Gaspar von Mercy (*Generalwachtmeister der Reiterei*), and Ruischenberg commanded the infantry (*Generalwachtmeister des Fussvolkes*).

---

20 Cosalky's and Wolf's regiments had 1,100 horse and 1,200 dragoons respectively in May, according to the *Mercure Français* of 1644, but Cosalky lost 100 to 120 men in the first battle against Rosen, then the 2 regiments lost 376 men and 500 prisoners in the second Battle at Hüfflingen on 4 June. Jean Henault (ed.) *Tome Premier de l'Histoire de Nostre Temps Sous le Regne du Très-Chrestien Roy de France & de Navarre, Louis XIX es années 1643 & 1644 ou Tome Vingt-cinquiesme du Mercure François es Mesmes Années 1643 et 1644* (Paris, 1648), vol.2, pp.399–400.

21 Heilmann, *Kriegsgefchichte von Bayern, Franken, Pfalz und Schwaben von 1506 bis 1651*, p.955.

THE BATTLE OF FRIBOURG 1644

A rare rear view of a Musketeer. Drawing by Anthonie Palamedesz, c. 1645 (Public Domain)

5

Preamble: 28 July

Situated at the foot of the Black Forest, five leagues east of Brisach, in a crescent-shaped valley, Fribourg is a strategic location. The plain on which the town nestles lies between high mountains to the east and the Mooswald marshland to the west. A stream, the Dreisam, waters the plain. The road from Brisach passes through a gorge before reaching Fribourg, skirting a high mountain: the Schönberg. The other roads leading to the city pass through deep valleys. Henri de Bessé described the area as follows:

> Fribourg lies at the foot of the Black Forest mountains. They widen out in the shape of a crescent, and in the middle of this area near Fribourg is a small plain bounded on the right by very high mountains and surrounded on the left by a marshy wood. This plain is watered by a small stream that runs alongside the wood and then falls to the left of Fribourg in a narrow valley cut by marshes and woods. Those coming from Brisach can only enter this plain through gorges at the foot of an almost inaccessible mountain that dominates it on all sides, and by the other roads, entry is even more difficult.[1]

On 28 July, Fribourg capitulated. At the head of 9,000 men, Turenne was the first to arrive on the scene. But faced with more than 15,000 Bavarians, he thought it prudent not to engage the enemy. He had been studying the terrain for more than a fortnight and had noted that Mercy had left the Schönberg, a strategic point dominating the plain to the south-west of Fribourg, unoccupied. Thinking he could take advantage of the enemy's negligence, he sent a battalion of 1,000 men, made up of the Montausier and Melun regiments, to take possession of it. But the perceptive Mercy saw the manoeuvre and sent about 20 musketeers to slow them down. A few exchanges of fire later, misjudging the size of the enemy force, the entire French battalion retreated in disarray. Turenne's plan was thwarted by a twist of fate. The surprise attack having failed, Mercy took advantage of the situation to occupy this key position. Disappointed, Turenne had the two ensigns that had confused the battalion broken. He abandoned his original

---

[1] Henri de Bessé, Sieur de la Chapelle Milon, *Relation des campagnes de Rocroi et Fribourg*, in Collection de Petits Classiques François (Paris: N. Delangle Editeur 1826), pp.93–94.

idea and decided to deploy his army 400 paces from the Schönberg, waiting for the Duc d'Enghien's army of 10,000 men.

The French Battle Plan

To reach Turenne as quickly as possible, Enghien had left his baggage and a large part of his artillery in Metz. From Metz, he took only 400 horses and the necessary artillery.

On 31 July, in Brisach, a council of war brought together the Duc d'Enghien, the *Maréchal* de Turenne, the *Maréchal* de Guiche, d'Aumont, d'Espenan, Tournon, d'Erlach, Governor of Brisach and Chouppes. The latter stated:

> *M.* de Turenne and *M.* d'Aumont were of the opinion that they should immediately march towards the enemy and fight them. They assured us that their camp was not entrenched, that they only had 6,000 horse and 10,000 infantry exhausted by the fatigue of the siege they had been conducting, instead with the armies of *M.* le Duc d'Enghien and *M.* de Turenne being united, we would find ourselves with 10,000 horse and 12,000 foot. The Duc d'Enghien, who breathed nothing but opportunities to make a name for himself, was delighted that his council had prevailed.[2]

The die was cast. The Duc d'Enghien had ammunition and wine distributed to all the soldiers, then, during the night, gave the order to leave.

On the night of 2/3 August, the Duc set off with Turenne to reconnoitre the area. But a surprise awaited them: 'When the Duc d'Enghien had examined the camp a little, he was very surprised to find it in a very different state to the one in which M. de Turenne had represented it to the council of war. It was entrenched by a good, well-palisaded line and defended by several redoubts and a small fort.'[3] He complained about this to Turenne. Embarrassed, the latter assured him that, during the reconnaissance carried out two days ago with 1,000 horse, there were no Bavarian entrenchments. Enghien then called a meeting of the council of war to decide on the battle plan:

> All the general officers, such as *Messrs* De Gramont [he was actually still only Compte de Guiche], de Palluau, d'Espenan, Marsin and the Comte de Tournon, readily acknowledged that *M.* de Turenne had wanted to embroil the Duc d'Enghien in a tricky affair. I made the same judgement; I believe that this prince was not the last to realise this. However, things being so far advanced that it was no longer possible to retrace his steps, the Duc d'Enghien took the decision to

---

2   Aymar de Chouppes, *Mémoires du Marquis de Chouppes, Lieutenant Général des Armées du Roi*, in Mémoires du Marquis de Chouppes, Lieutenant Général des armées du Roi suivis des Mémoires Duc de Navailles et de la Valette pair et Maréchal de France et Gouverneur de Monseigneur le Duc de Chartres (Paris: J. Techener, 1861),.68–69.

3   Chouppes, *Mémoires du Marquis de Chouppes, Lieutenant Général des Armées du Roi,* pp.70.

PREAMBLE: 28 JULY

Thirty Years' War period tents, watercolour by K. A. Wilke. (Bibliothèque Universitaire de Lausanne, photo by the author)

assemble the council of war to deliberate on the best place to make the attack. *Maréchal* de Turenne was present at the council. Everyone was of the opinion that the attack was not practicable from the side facing our camp; but when it came to determining precisely where the attack should be made, the council was divided into I don't know how many opinions.[4]

D'Erlach then suggested to the Duc that he should lead his attack via Langen Denzlingen and the Val Saint-Pierre, in order to avoid too strong a position while cutting off the Bavarian lines of communication. The Governor of

---

4   Chouppes, *Mémoires du Marquis de Chouppes, Lieutenant Général des Armées du Roi*, pp.70–71.

Brisach's knowledge of the area earned him the approval of the council, with the exception of Espenan. According to de Chouppes, Turenne then supported Espenan, saying, according to de Chouppes:

> it would be shameful for the Duc to have come so close to the enemies without fighting them, and that all those who were servants of His Highness should not hesitate to advise him to give battle now, without seeking detours and delays. [he then asserted that] not so much-needed to be said to a prince such as the Duc d'Enghien to make him resolve to fight. The battle was therefore resolved. The *Maréchal* de Turenne was delighted.[5]

For his part, the *Maréchal* de Guiche states that he agreed with d'Erlach and describes the scene:

> The *Maréchal* de Guiche was quite in favour of this advice, which seemed to him to be fair and based on reason; but the *Maréchal* de Turenne assured us that he had had a valley recognised which was not entrenched, through which his troops would attack the enemies while those of the Duc d'Enghien would attack the entrenchments (which would cause them great embarrassment), and his advice was followed.[6]

However, Ramsay does not share these two versions of events. According to him, it was Turenne who seems to have proposed leading the army through Langen Dentzlingen to Val Saint-Pierre and d'Erlach and de Guiche would have agreed with him.

> The Duc d'Enghien alone absolutely wanted the enemy to be attacked in their entrenchments: he therefore went himself to reconnoitre the Bavarian camp and the neighbouring places with the Vicomte, who showed him a defile, by which part of his army could take them by the left flank, while the other part would attack by the front and right flank.[7]

The *Gazette Renaudot* did not mention this incident, merely reporting that Enghien and Turenne had gone to reconnoitre the enemy, 'of whom, however, we were unable to gain much knowledge, being posted in a place where it was very difficult to see the particulars, unless we marched there with the whole army.'[8]

We do not know what actually happened at this council. De Chouppes and de Guiche affirmed that the proposal came from d'Erlach and that Turenne did not support it. According to Chéruel, Vittorio Siri confirmed this position.[9]

---

5   Chouppes, *Mémoires du Marquis de Chouppes, Lieutenant Général des Armées du Roi*, p.71.
6   Gramont, *Mémoires du Maréchal de Gramont*, tome 7, p.256.
7   Ramsay, *Histoire du Vicomte de Turenne, Maréchal-Général des Armées du Roy*, p.122.
8   Renaudot, *Recueil des Gazettes et Nouvelles Ordinaires et autres relations des choses avenues toute l'année mille six cents quarante-quatre*, p.662.
9   Adolphe Chéruel, *Histoire de France pendant la minorité de Louis XIV* (Paris: Hachette, 1879), p.302.

For his part, Turenne does not mention this advice in his Mémoires.[10] Only the Baron de Sirot confirms Ramsay's version: 'the *Maréchal* de Turenne did well to point out to him the perils of the attack he wished to undertake and that he would run the risk of losing all his troops …. But allow me to try to win over the enemy's rear, so as to divert their forces and prevent them from falling on you,' Turenne is said to have told Enghien,[11] but neither Ramsay nor Sirot were present at this council of war.

Be that as it may, Enghien was well aware of the difficulties of such an undertaking, and the proposal for a double attack from the west and south was therefore decided. The following arrangements were made: Enghien would make a frontal attack on the redoubts, leaving the fort on his left, while Turenne would go around the mountain to the south and east, taking the small road from Ehrenkirchen via Sölden, Wittnau and Merzhausen:

> The Vicomte de Turenne was to attack the clump of trees defending the valley, and provided that the two attacks were made at the same time, there was reason to hope that the enemy, being separated in two places, would be unable to defend himself; and that if he were forced to the side of the ravine, with the Duc d'Enghien coming from the heights and the Vicomte de Turenne entering the plain at the same time, Mercy would not be able to resist them.[12]

Ramsay describes the plan in these terms: The Duc d'Enghien:

> resolved to go himself with the French army to chase the Bavarians off the mountain, gain the high ground and then descend to attack them in their camp, while the Vicomte would go with the Weimarian troops to flank them through the defile. As they had a big turn to make, it was decided that the Prince [editor's note: the Duc and not the Prince] would not attack until three hours before sunset, so that the two attacks could take place at the same time.[13]

This last provision is confirmed by Turenne's Memoirs:

> M. d'Enghien resolved to attack with his army posts where the enemy had three or four regiments of infantry at the head of his camp on the heights, and that M. de Turenne would go, with the troops he commanded, through the woods and mountains, to try to enter the plain where the enemy was, and take him by the flank. It was decided to attack about three hours before dark. The situation of the country meant that the armies had to be two hours apart when passing through the mountains, so that it was only at night that they could hear each other's actions.[14]

---

10 Marichal, *Mémoires du Maréchal de Turenne*, p.13.
11 Letouf, *Mémoires et la vie de messire Claude de Letouf, chevalier baron de Sirot*, p.106.
12 Bessé, *Relation des Campagnes de Rocroi et Fribourg*, p.97.
13 Ramsay, *Histoire du Vicomte de Turenne, Maréchal-Général des Armées du Roy*, p.124.
14 Marichal, *Mémoires du Maréchal de Turenne*, p.13.

THE BATTLE OF FRIBOURG 1644

August 3, 1644: The plan

The version by the Marquis de Chouppes adds details and differs slightly as regards the time: he does not write three hours before nightfall, which would mean a little past four o'clock in the afternoon, but three o'clock in the afternoon:

> It was decided that the two armies together would begin the attack at three o'clock in the afternoon; and so that the two armies would attack at precisely the same moment, *Mr* le Duc d'Enghien set two watches to the same time; he gave one to Mr de Turenne and kept the other.[15]

Thus the success of the plan depended on the coordination of the two assaults.

Mercy, making the most of the time, had effectively placed his army in an advantageous position. His camp backed onto a stream, and where there were no woods or marshes to protect his regiments, he had constructed entrenchments. Thus, on the slope that runs down to the plain, above the vineyards, there was a palisaded fort, defended by 600 men and five guns, followed by a series of redoubts spaced 200 paces apart, covered with barricades, abattis and chevaux de frise, all the way to the summit. Ramsay describes this position as:

> On the slope of this height, on the French side, he [Mercy] had a palisaded fort made, where he placed six hundred men with artillery. To make access more difficult, he had a large number of trees felled all along this work, the branches of which, half-cut and bristling in all directions, served as chevaux de frise. Between the height at the head of the enemy camp and the mountains that dominated the left side coming from Fribourg was the defile, which could only be reached by making a long detour. Mercy also had entrenchments at the entrance to the defile, and had blocked it with felled fir trees; he had also garrisoned the woods to the right and left with infantry; so that he did not imagine that anyone could ever attempt this passage, which he believed he had made impassable.[16]

This was a formidable defensive position, the fruit of several days' work. In a letter sent to Piccolomini, Mercy wrote that his council of war, 'decided to maintain the army in the positions it occupied and to wait there for the enemy.'[17] The Bavarian general seriously doubted that it would be possible to break through the valley on his left flank because, by his own assessment, the paths were impassable and 'the mountain was covered with tall trees and thick bushes.'[18]

---

15   Chouppes, *Mémoires du Marquis de Chouppes, Lieutenant Général des Armées du Roi*, pp.71–72.
16   Ramsay, *Histoire du Vicomte de Turenne, Maréchal-Général des Armées du Roy*, pp.122–123.
17   Duc d'Aumale, *Histoire des princes de Condé pendant les XVIe et XVIIe siècles*, vol. 4, pp.603–604.
18   Duc d'Aumale, *Histoire des princes de Condé pendant les XVIe et XVIIe siècles*, vol. 4, pp.603–604.

THE BATTLE OF FRIBOURG 1644

General Officer watching the army move past. Note the 'Croat' fashion of headwear on the staff officer behind him and on the trumpeter at right, this may indicate that they are Croats but is more likely a fashionable affectation (hussar uniforms attracted a similar affectation in later centuries). Also notable is the movement of the column with flank guards and additionally what looks like a general officer's carriage. Engraving by Stephano Della Bella (courtesy of Metropolitan Museum of Art, New York, collection)

A. Maximilian von Bayern, 1620. watercolour by K. A. Wilke.
(Bibliothèque Universitaire de Lausanne, photo by the author)
See Colour Plate Commentaries for further information.

B. Jan von Werth, watercolour by K. A. Wilke.
(Bibliothèque Universitaire de Lausanne, photo by the author)
See Colour Plate Commentaries for further information.

C. Bavarian trumpeter watercolour by K. A. Wilke.
(Bibliothèque Universitaire de Lausanne, photo by the author)
See Colour Plate Commentaries for further information.

D. Bavarian early and late Cuirassiers watercolour by K. A. Wilke.
(Bibliothèque Universitaire de Lausanne, photo by the author)
See Colour Plate Commentaries for further information.

E. Louis II de Bourbon, Duc d'Enghien, watercolour by K. A. Wilke.
(Bibliothèque Universitaire de Lausanne, photo by the author)
See Colour Plate Commentaries for further information.

F. Henri de La Tour d'Auvergne, vicomte de Turenne, Watercolour by K. A. Wilke.
(Bibliothèque Universitaire de Lausanne, photo by the author)
See Colour Plate Commentaries for further information.

G. French infantry c. **1644: Top, musketeer and types of headwear. Bottom from left to right: An anspessadoe, an ensign and a pikeman. Watercolour by K. A. Wilke.**
(Bibliothèque Universitaire de Lausanne, photo by the author)
See Colour Plate Commentaries for further information.

H. French infantry: From left to right: an officer c. **1640, an officer** c. **1645, an ensign and a fifer. Watercolour by K. A. Wilke.**
(Bibliothèque Universitaire de Lausanne, photo by the author)
See Colour Plate Commentaries for further information.

I. French infantry *c.* **1644: From left to right: Pikeman, drummer from the** *Gardes Françaises* **and** *petardier* **(fireworker). Watercolour by K. A. Wilke.**
(Bibliothèque Universitaire de Lausanne, photo by the author)
See Colour Plate Commentaries for further information.

J. French cavalry: From left to right: A mounted fusilier from Régiment de Condé cavalerie c. **1646, trumpeter from Régiment de Turenne cavalerie** c. **1644. watercolour by K. A. Wilke.**
(Bibliothèque Universitaire de Lausanne, photo by the author)
See Colour Plate Commentaries for further information.

K. Generic Dutch and German cavalry of the 1640s, watercolour by K. A. Wilke.
(Bibliothèque Universitaire de Lausanne, photo by the author)
See Colour Plate Commentaries for further information.

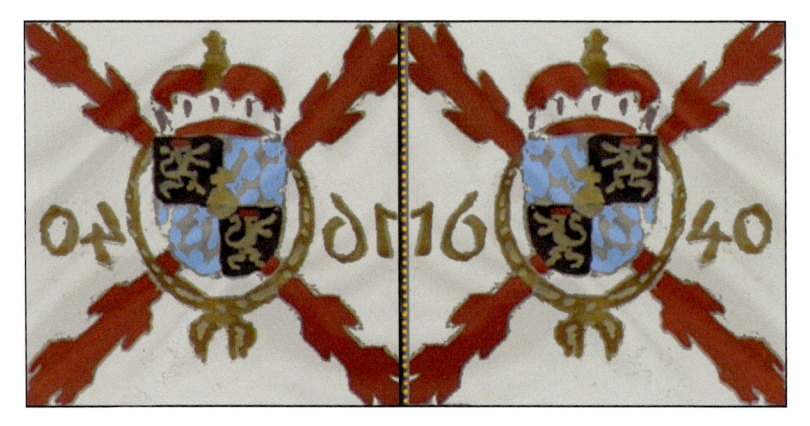

L1. Bavarian Colour from an old engraving depicting Mercy's death at Alerheim in 1645 (illustration by K. A. Wilke). Note the two following colours are from the same regiment. Some of Mercy's regiments at Fribourg were also present at Alerheim - IR Gold, Mercy, Rouyer, Ruischenberg and Winterscheid.

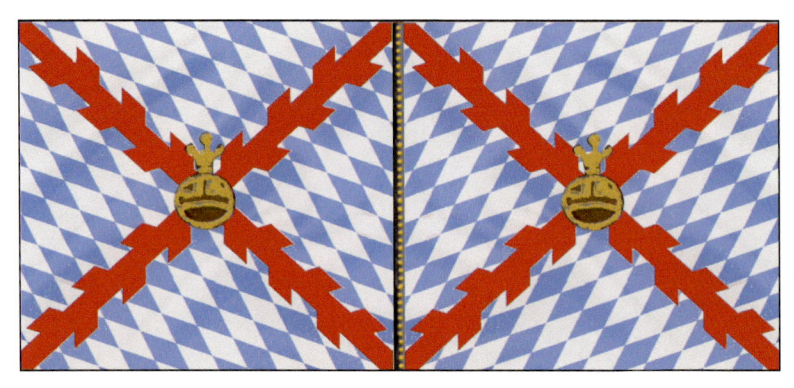

L2. Bavarian Colour from an old engraving depicting Mercy's death at Alerheim in 1645, (illustration by K. A. Wilke). Note the preceding and the following colour are from the same regiment.

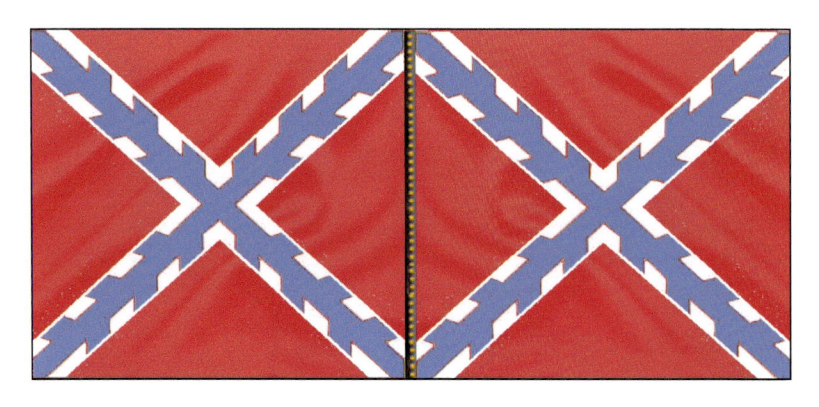

L3. Bavarian Colour from an old engraving depicting Mercy's death at Alerheim (1645), (illustration by K. A. Wilke). Note this and the preceding two colours are from the same regiment.

L4. Bavarian Colour from an old engraving depicting Mercy's death at Alerheim (1645), (illustration by K. A. Wilke). Note this and the following two colours are from the same regiment.

See Colour Plate Commentaries for further information.

M1. Bavarian Colour from an old engraving depicting Mercy's death at Alerheim in 1645, (illustration by K. A. Wilke). Note the preceding and the following colour are from the same regiment.

M2. Bavarian Colour from an old engraving depicting Mercy's death at Allerheim (1645), (illustration by K. A. Wilke). Note this and the preceding two colours are from the same regiment.

M3. Colour identified as Bavarian in the Stockholm Armémuseum, reference 833-VIII-I 8e delen.

M4. French standard of Turenne's Regiment of Horse, watercolour by K. A. Wilke (Author's artwork)

See Colour Plate Commentaries for further information.

XIII

N1. French colour of a Weimarian Regiment of Foot, watercolour by K. A. Wilke (Author's artwork)

N2. French Colour of Mazarin-Italien Regiment of Foot (Author's artwork)

N3. French Colour of Montausier Regiment of Foot (Author's artwork)

N4. French Colour of Enghien Regiment of Foot (Author's artwork)

N5. French Colour of La Reine-Mère (later La Couronne) Regiment of Foot (Author's artwork)

See Colour Plate Commentaries for further information.

6

The Attack by the Duc d'Enghien, 3 August 1644

The Bavarian infantry was under the command of *General Wachtmeister* von Ruischenberg. Four regiments were deployed on the western slopes of the Schönberg, facing the Army of Champagne. To the north and west of Uffhausen, the Winterscheid regiment held the entrenchments in front of Wendlingen. Further south, 600 men of the Hasslang regiment occupied the fort called Sternschanze. Below, Fugger defended the first redoubt and Holz the second of the two redoubts on the slopes of the Bohl. On the other side, to the north-east of the Schönberg, Rouyer's regiment blocked the access around the mountain to the east, where Turenne was due to emerge. Behind Uffhausen, on the plain between the Schönberg and Fribourg, Mercy kept the Mercy, Ruischenberg, Gold and Miehr regiments in reserve. The Enschering regiment was in Fribourg. According to Schaufler, only half the regiment, i.e. about 300 men, with 40 cavalry from Cosalky's regiment of mounted harquebusiers.[1] Each regiment formed a battalion of 600 to 700 men on average.[2] The Wahl regiment was missing from these arrangements. Hans-Helmut Schaufler placed it on the Schönberg, along with the Wintersheid, Holz and Hasslang regiments. He also placed the Fugger regiment with the reserve, alongside the Mercy, Gold and Miehr regiments, but did not mention the position of the Ruischenberg regiment.[3] The artillery, with the exception of the guns occupying the Sternschanze, was distributed among the redoubts. Finally, Jean de Werth's cavalry was deployed further north, between Haslach and Saint-Georges, protecting the north-west access to the marshes. The placement of Rouyer's regiment on his left flank showed that Mercy did not rule out the possibility of an attempt to attack the area.

While waiting for the time of the attack, set for three o'clock in the afternoon on Wednesday (or four o'clock in the version of the Marquis de Chouppes), Enghien asked d'Espenan, in charge of the vanguard, to draw up

---

1   Schaufler, *Die Schlacht bei Freiburg im Breisgau 1644*, p.75.
2   August Lufft, *Die Schlachten bei Freiburg im August 1644* (Freiburg und Tübingen, 1882), pp.43–44.
3   Schaufler, *Die Schlacht bei Freiburg im Breisgau 1644*, p.75.

THE BATTLE OF FRIBOURG 1644

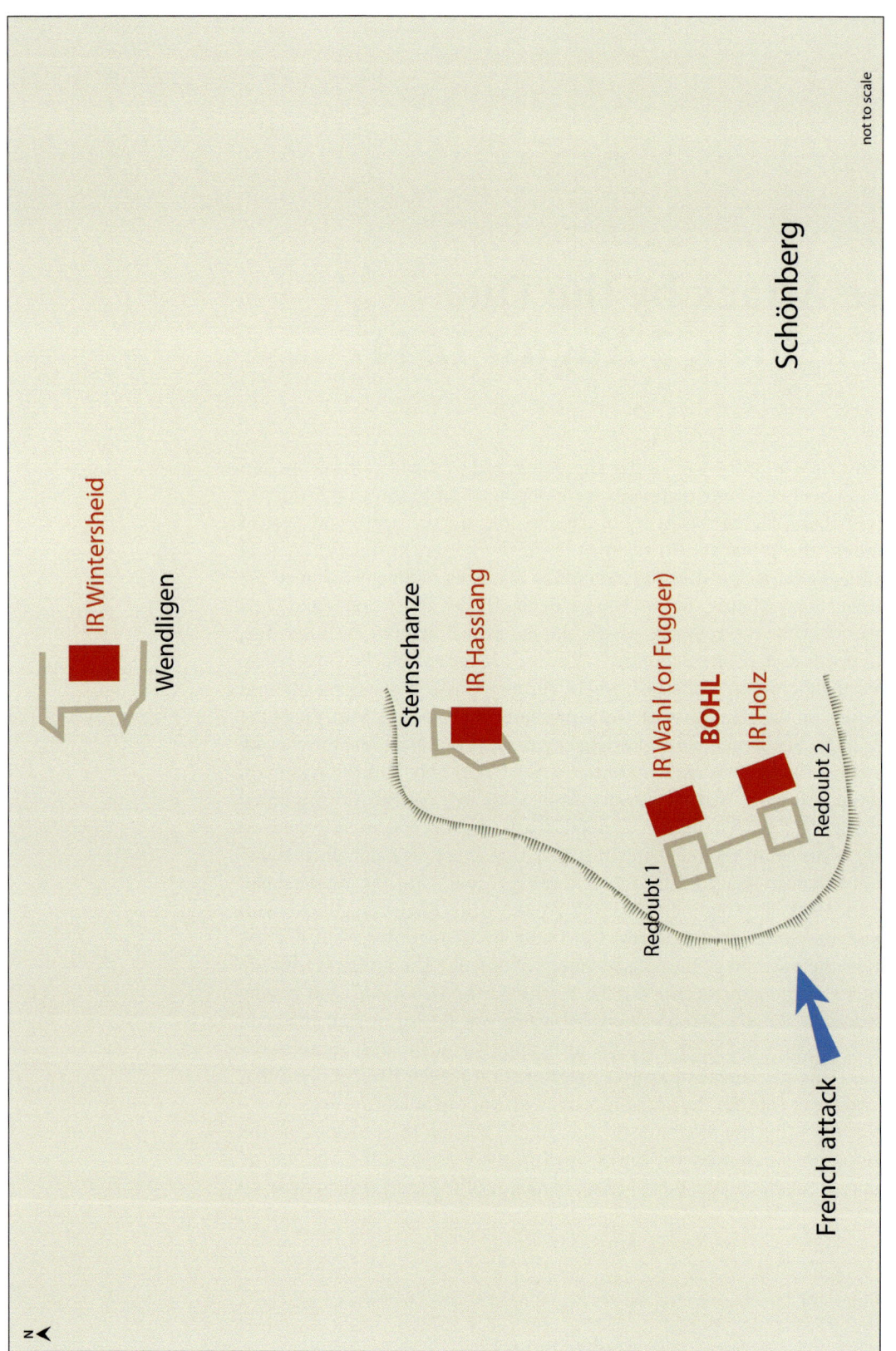

Bavarian deployment

not to scale

Schönberg

IR Wintersheid
Wendligen

Sternschanze
IR Hasslang

IR Wahl (or Fugger)
BOHL
IR Holz

Redoubt 1
Redoubt 2

French attack

THE ATTACK BY THE DUC D'ENGHIEN, 3 AUGUST 1644

his troops for the attack. The infantry consisted of six battalions of 800 men each. Espenan was to lead the two battalions from Persan and Enghien on the right, Persan on the right and Enghien on the left.[4] He would be followed by the two French battalions of Conti and Mazarin, led by the Compte de Tournon.[5] *Maréchal* de Guiche (who did not become *Maréchal* de Gramont until 1648) wrote in his *Mémoires* that 'there were the two regiments of Conti and Mazarin there, which were good and very strong, and that he was going to lead them to attack the entrenchment in front of him.'[6] The Duc d'Enghien reserved the use of the last two battalions, made up of the Le Havre and Bussy regiments under the command of Marsin,[7] to act accordingly.

Palluau was to support the attack with the Enghien cavalry regiment. Further north, the companies of *gendarmes* and several squadrons of *chevau-légers* were placed at the entrance to the plain, 'in a very tight spot,'[8] to prevent the Bavarian cavalry from outflanking the attack. Finally, Enghien ordered de Chouppes to place the artillery at the most advantageous points. Given the quality of the enemy entrenchments, this was a delicate task, but the Marquis nevertheless managed to 'position the artillery in such a way that it would serve well.'[9]

To reach the enemy line, the French had to climb a steep slope through a vineyard, 'in which there were four-foot-high walls from space to space, supporting the land,'[10] a sort of entrenchment for the Bavarians.

At the agreed time, Espenan launched the attack: climbing the slope, crossing the vines, but reaching the enemy entrenchments in disarray and under terrible fire from the Holz and Wahl (or Fugger if we follow August Lufft) regiments, his men were unable to break through the enemy defences. 'Although he did everything that could be expected of a man of his courage, he was unable to force them'[11] said de Chouppes. It was then that d'Espenan decided to 'scout along the enemy line'[12] to find a more favourable passage. Enghien became impatient, he saw that most of his front line had not managed to break through the enemy entrenchments, even though a few of them appeared to have done so. His men remained stuck in their positions, neither retreating nor attacking. It was at this point that he saw d'Espenan's manoeuvre. If we are to believe de Chouppes, the young Duke became enraged and dismounted, followed by his officers and volunteers. *Maréchal* de Guiche tried to dissuade him.

The official report of the battle notes only that Enghien, having 'himself recognised that it was impossible to force this place, judged that the

---

4 Renaudot, *Recueil des Gazettes et Nouvelles Ordinaires et Extraordinaires et autres relations des choses avenues toute l'année mille six cents quarante-quatre*, p.663.
5 Bessé, Sieur de la Chapelle Milon, *Relation des Campagnes de Rocroi et Fribourg*, in Collection de Petits Classiques François, p.98.
6 Gramont, *Mémoires du Maréchal de Gramont*, tome 7, p.256.
7 Ramsay, *Histoire du Vicomte de Turenne, Maréchal-Général des Armées du Roy*, pp.124–125.
8 Ramsay, *Histoire du Vicomte de Turenne, Maréchal-Général des Armées du Roy*, p.125.
9 Chouppes, *Mémoires du Marquis de Chouppes, Lieutenant Général des Armées du Roi*, p.72.
10 Ramsay, *Histoire du Vicomte de Turenne, Maréchal-Général des Armées du Roy*, p.125.
11 Chouppes, *Mémoires du Marquis de Chouppes, Lieutenant Général des Armées du Roi*, p.72.
12 Chouppes, *Mémoires du Marquis de Chouppes, Lieutenant Général des Armées du Roi*, p.72.

THE BATTLE OF FRIBOURG 1644

Overall dispositions of the units on 3 August, 1644

THE ATTACK BY THE DUC D'ENGHIEN, 3 AUGUST 1644

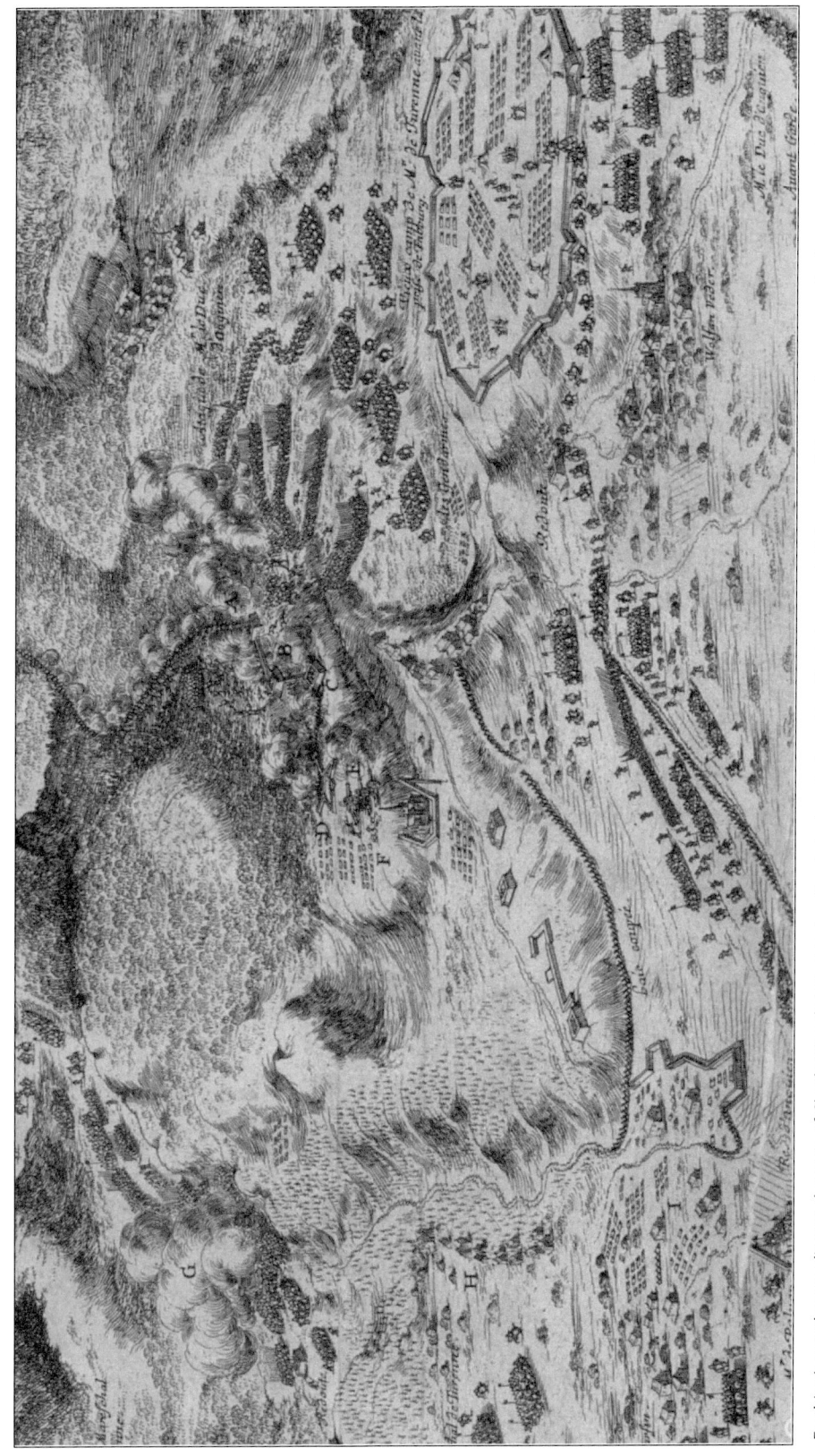

Enghien's attack according to the map of Charles Nicolas Cochin, *Les Combats donnés devant la ville et chateau de Fribourg en Brisgau et les attaques des forts et retranchements faictz au Tour d'icelle par l'armée Bavaroise et les avantages remportés sur ladicte Armée par Monseigneur le Duc d'Anguien les 3, 5 et le 10 Aoust 1644* (BNF)

success of his enterprise depended only on taking the enemy line at the centre.'[13] He therefore decided to launch the second attack with what remained of the first regiments, supported on their left by the second brigade. Henri de Bessé explained the decision to launch this second attack as follows:

> First of all, it seemed foolhardy to undertake, with two thousand men who had given up fighting, to force three thousand who were well entrenched and proud of the advantage they had just won. But it was impossible to free those who had passed the first entrenchment of fir trees in any other way, because by abandoning them, the Duc d'Enghien would withdraw with the displeasure of having failed in his undertaking and sacrificed the best part of his infantry in no useful way; in addition, the entire Bavarian army would have fallen into the arms of the Vicomte de Turenne, having nothing left to defend against but himself.[14]

This second attack was led by the Count de Tournon's brigade. Jacques de Castelnau-Mauvissière, *mestre de camp*, led the Mazarin-Français regiment, with, on his left, the Conti regiment commanded by Saint Point. Before leading the battalions, Enghien ordered the Compte de Tournon to detach some musketeers in readiness for the attack. Then, followed by gentlemen volunteers, he led the two battalions, each at a different redoubt, De Choupples wrote:

French musketeer attacking, watercolour by K. A. Wilke. (Bibliothèque Universitaire de Lausanne, photo by the author)

---

13   Bessé, *Relation des Campagnes de Rocroi et Fribourg*, p.100.
14   Bessé, *Relation des Campagnes de Rocroi et Fribourg*, pp.100–101.

THE ATTACK BY THE DUC D'ENGHIEN, 3 AUGUST 1644

The redoubts were attacked with all the valour imaginable; they defended so stubbornly that they could only be taken by force and after more than fourteen hundred men and enemies had been killed in each.[15]

The account probably inflates the enemy losses. De Guiche, in his Mémoires, gives an even exaggerated account of these losses while probably embellishing his own role and that of the Duc d'Enghien:

For this purpose he [de Guiche] dismounted and marched straight to the entrenchment: when the Duc d'Enghien saw him, he did the same thing; and a gentleman of the *Maréchal*'s wanted to prevent him from doing so, it was not long before he gave him a sword in the stomach. Finally, to shorten the narrative, the Duc d'Enghien and the *Maréchal* de Guiche both marched close to the entrenchment and took it with an audacity that cannot be imagined, after coming under terrible fire. It was there that the enemies lost, without exaggeration, more than three thousand men who were killed on the square, and who were given no quarter, having defended themselves to the last extremity, for they were the elite of the Emperor's infantry.[16]

Maréchal de Guiche, watercolour by K. A. Wilke. (Bibliothèque Universitaire de Lausanne, photo by the author)

---

15 Chouppes, *Mémoires du Marquis de Chouppes, Lieutenant Général des Armées du Roi,* p.73.
16 Gramont, *Mémoires du Maréchal de Gramont,* tome 7, p.256. This figure of 'three thousand men killed' is, of course, greatly exaggerated: The four regiments lined up – Winterscheid, Fugger, Holz and Hasslang – totalled around 2,600 men at the start of the battle. If de Guiche and de Chouppes are to be believed, they would have been totally destroyed. In reality, the two redoubts were each occupied by a regiment of fewer than 700 men. Total losses, if the two regiments were annihilated, could therefore not have exceeded 1,400 men.

THE BATTLE OF FRIBOURG 1644

The Bavarian regiments Holz and Wahl (or Fugger) suffered the most, caught in the rear by the men of the Persan regiment. One redoubt was taken by the Mazarin regiment, a second by Conti's regiment. According to Mercy, 'repulsed twice with losses, a third attack made him [Enghien] master of a fort.'[17] Fearing that he would be shot, the Bavarian general ordered Ruischenberg to withdraw to the mountains, and as night fell and rain began to fall, the French took up positions in the entrenchments.

Enghien took stock of the situation: some of his infantry were casualties on the battlefield and the rest of his men were off in pursuit of the fugitives, and the Sternschanze fort, equipped with artillery, was still in Bavarian possession. Fortunately, nightfall protected his troops from a possible counter-attack. Enghien then regrouped his infantry, brought the cavalry up to the occupied heights and ordered de Chouppes to supply the redoubts with artillery before dawn. The operation was tricky: the Sternschanze fort overlooked the redoubts. Well equipped with artillery, its occupants would be able to silence the French guns. De Chouppes decided to send a sergeant and ten musketeers to reconnoitre the fort. Fortunately, and to his surprise, the fort had been abandoned by the enemy. The *Gazette* claimed that it was the Comte de Tournon, who was in charge of the assault.[18]

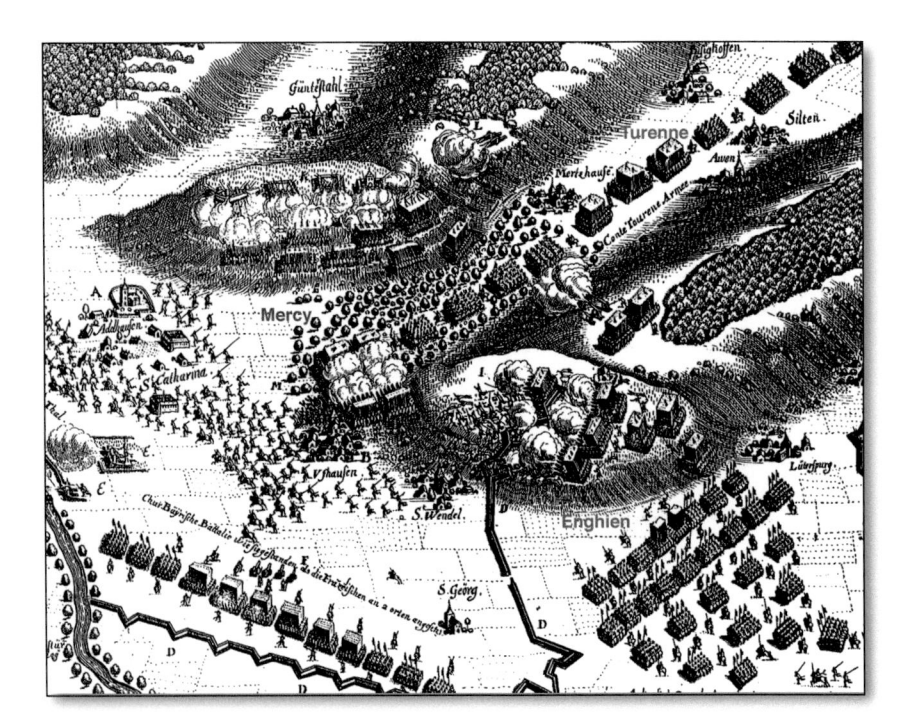

French attack of 3 August according to the *Theatrum Europaeum*

De Chouppes then went to report to the Duc d'Enghien. He found him in one of the redoubts, sleeping in the company of the Comte de Guiche, the

---

17 Duc d'Aumale, *Histoire des princes de Condé pendant les XVIe et XVIIe siècles*, vol. 4, p.605.
18 Renaudot, *Recueil des Gazettes et Nouvelles Ordinaires et Extraordinaires et autres relations des choses avenues toute l'année mille six cents quarante-quatre*, p.664.

two men wrapped in their coats. He woke them and told them that the fort had been taken, and the three men hurried off to ascertain the situation. As day broke, they realised that the enemy had taken advantage of the night to withdraw. Mercy, fearing that the French would bypass him, had thought it prudent to withdraw the infantry and artillery from Ruischenberg to a second mountain, the Josephberg, 'this plan was carried out without us [the Bavarians] being worried or pursued by the enemy.'[19]

Later, admiring the effort made by the French infantry, Mercy could not help expressing his admiration to the Baron de Sirot, who had been his prisoner since Tuttlingen. Mercy told him:

> From now on, I will believe your predictions, and it can be said that the French are the best soldiers in the world. We were entrenched in places where I thought only birds could get close; we had made the whole mountain uncomfortable with the wooden abatis that we had had poured down the slope; we had fortified ourselves in various places and were covered with several forts. These difficulties did not prevent Enghien from dislodging us and neither blood nor carnage could stop his impetuosity. He gave his all like a lion, and the magnitude of the peril only increased his courage. In truth, only the French can undertake such things; other nations are not capable of it, and it takes more than human virtue to succeed in such undertakings.... Whatever it was, they dislodged us from a place we thought inaccessible, and as actions in war can only be judged by good or bad successes, we can say that the Duc d'Enghien did one that posterity will regard as a prodigy.[20]

Turenne in action

Maréchal de Turenne's orders were to outflank the Bavarians. To do this, he had to take a valley called the Bannstein Pass, which lies between the Schönberg and the heights of Fribourg. The pass was narrow and heavily wooded.

Mercy, although he thought the western defences of this mountain impassable, had reinforced the defences of the valley on that side. As soon as his outposts warned him of the attack, he himself led the Fugger, Miehr, Gold and Mercy regiments there, as well as two cavalry squadrons, to oppose Turenne's forces. According to Bessé, 'there was enough space behind the entrenchment to put the troops in battle, and all the Bavarian cavalry could support the line without breaking its squadrons.'[21]

Turenne had to lead his men along near-impassable paths, through bushes and forest. With foresight, he provided some peasants with axes to clear a path for him. His vanguard consisted of a thousand musketeers led by Roqueservières, followed by the Weimarian brigade led by Nettancourt.

---

19 Duc d'Aumale, *Histoire des princes de Condé pendant les XVIe et XVIIe siècles* (Paris: Calmann Lévy, 1886), vol. 4, p.605.
20 Letouf, *Mémoires et la vie de messire Claude de Letouf, chevalier baron de Sirot*, pp.109–110.
21 Bessé, *Relation des Campagnes de Rocroi et Fribourg*, pp.103–104.

THE BATTLE OF FRIBOURG 1644

French foot, from an engraving of the siege of Rosas (Monasterio de Piedra, Spain)

Further to the right, d'Aumont led the French infantry brigades and cavalry along a path that led straight to the plain.

The pass was held by companies of the Rouyer regiment. The outposts were taken one by one, but the French progress was much slower than expected. They did, however, manage to break through to the main entrenchment. Thus slowed down, Turenne did not reach the barricades until around five o'clock. To carry out his attack, he ordered d'Aumont to deploy two brigades: one made up of the Montauzier and la Couronne regiments and the other made up of the Aubeterre and Tot regiments. These battalions would flank the Weimarian brigade of the Hattstein, Bernhold and Schmidtberg regiments.

The Franco-Weimarians launched a vigorous attack, which came up against the Bavarian defences. Ramsay described the fierceness of the fighting:

> [Turenne had to] fight new battles at every step, to flush out the infantry lodged on the right and left... but he pushed the enemy so hard that he took control of the passage, crossed all the ditches and ravines that traversed it, and penetrated as far as the wound at the end of the day. As the Duc d'Enghien had just ceased fighting, Mercy turned his main forces against the Vicomte: the troops remained at a distance of forty paces, fighting each other: heavy rain fell, and the darkness of the night increased the horrors of the place, which was only lit by the continuous fire of the musketry.[22]

---

22 Ramsay, *Histoire du Vicomte de Turenne, Maréchal-Général des Armées du Roy*, pp.127–128.

THE ATTACK BY THE DUC D'ENGHIEN, 3 AUGUST 1644

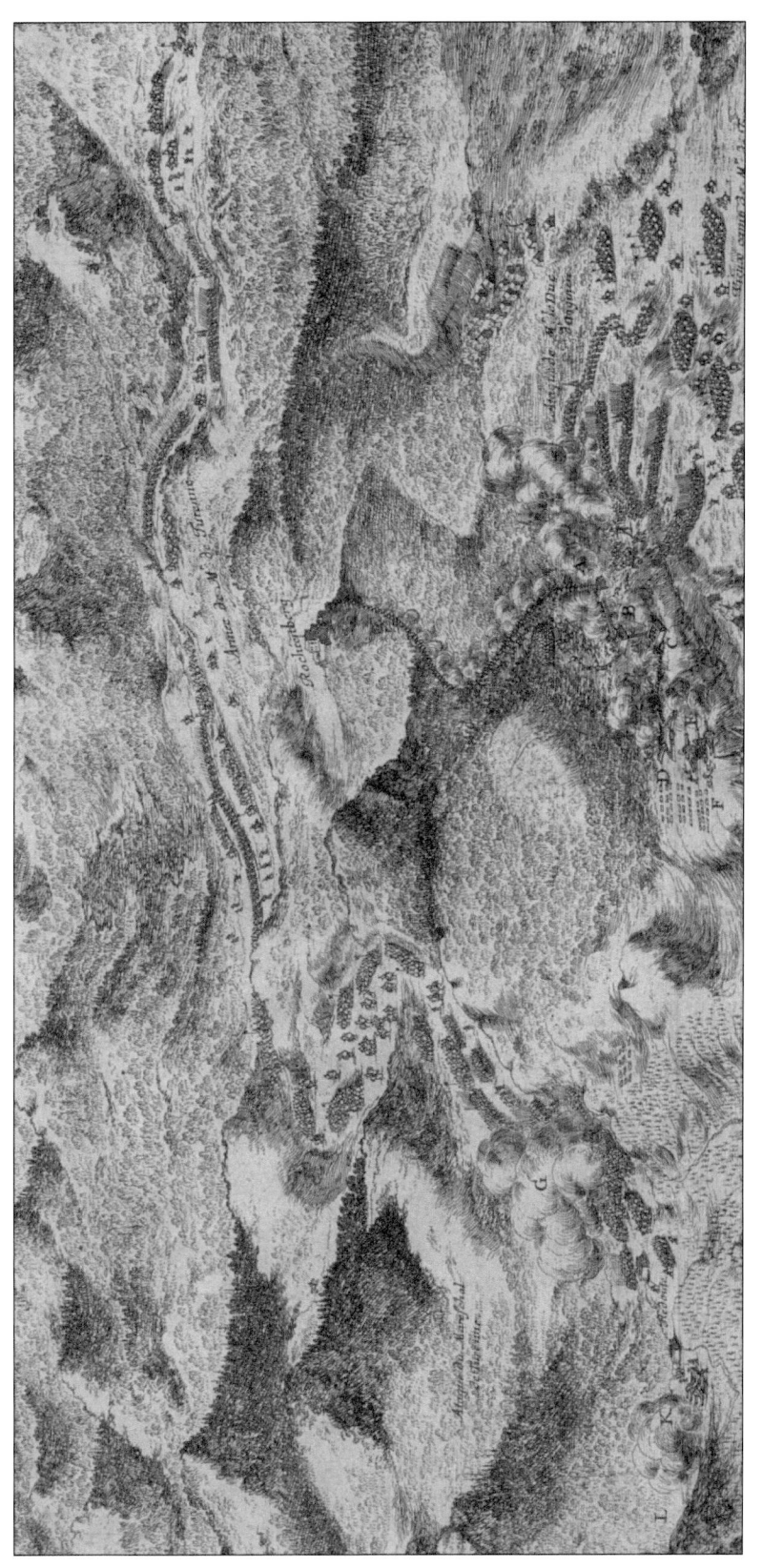

Turenne's attack according to the map of Charles Nicolas Cochin, *Les Combats donnés devant la ville et chasteau de Fribourg en Brisgau et les attaques des forts et retranchements faictz au Tour d'icelle par l'armée Bavaroise et les avantages remportés sur ladicte Armée par Monseigneur le Duc d'Anguien les 3, 5 et le 10 Aoust 1644* (BNF)

It seemed that only Rosen, at the head of two companies, managed to get through the hedge protecting the Bavarians. At the leading edge of the attack, Roqueservière was mortally wounded and d'Aumont took his place. His determination, despite a wound to the thigh, kept the French line in position, repelling the Bavarian counterattacks, probably from the Ruischenberg, Gold, Miehr and Fugger regiments. The fighting was intense. Hattstein was killed and Aubeterre was wounded twice. Finally, the two opponents came to a standstill, face to face, 'the Bavarians no longer daring to come to blows against these regiments who were waiting for them with their pikes, and the French not daring to enter further into the plain, having no cavalry to support them.'[23] According to Ramsay, the action lasted almost seven hours.

The fighting then turned into skirmishing that lasted most of the night. Shortly before daybreak, the French heard the enemy's musketry fade. In reality, the Bavarians were already gone. At four o'clock in the morning, hearing that the western redoubts had been taken, Mercy had decided to retreat. He left only a screen of musketeers to cover his withdrawal. De Guiche noted that:

> …nonetheless realising that the entrenchment had been taken, *General* Mercy, who commanded the Army of Bavaria, withdrew his troops and his cannon with an order that cannot be admired enough, and that same night posted himself on the Black Mountain near Fribourg, where, as he had no time to entrench himself, in the short time he was left, he made a large abatis of trees.[24]

All observers praised *Maréchal* Turenne's efforts. In his account of the battle, Bessé wrote:

> [he] showed on this occasion all that the valour and conduct of a great captain can do to overcome the disadvantage of numbers and location.[25]

De Guiche agreed, and finally, Mercy himself wrote:

> …as ardent as ever, Turenne attacked us with great fury to force a passage; but he found such resistance from us that his fight lasted all night, from five o'clock in the evening until four o'clock in the morning, and even longer, under continuous musket fire. The enemy was repulsed several times and our troops held on to the position: a French colonel was captured along with some ensigns; two small flags fell into our hands; Colonel Hatztein died on the spot.[26]

---

23   Marichal, *Mémoires du Maréchal de Turenne*, p.14.
24   Gramont, *Mémoires du Maréchal de Gramont,* tome 7, pp.256–257.
25   Bessé, *Relation des Campagnes de Rocroi et Fribourg*, p.104.
26   Duc d'Aumale, *Histoire des princes de Condé pendant les XVIe et XVIIe siècles*, vol. 4, pp.604–605.

THE ATTACK BY THE DUC D'ENGHIEN, 3 AUGUST 1644

The Opponents Catch Their Breath

Thursday 4 August was used to penetrate the enemy lines, reconnoitre, recover strength and prepare for a new offensive. But the French were in for a big surprise – in less than six hours, Mercy had managed to skilfully withdraw his troops near Fribourg, to a second line of defences placed on the Josephsberg,[27] a hill 340 metres above sea level. The new line stretched from Merzhausen in the south to Adelhausen in the north, a village separated from Fribourg by the river Dreisam. A plateau bordered by a small wood to the north crowned the Josephberg. Bessé described it as 'a mountain that is not extremely steep up to a third of its height, but the rest is very steep,' and he pointed out that this solid terrain was capable of holding 'three or four thousand men in battle.'[28] On the slopes facing west, and therefore facing the French troops, there were vineyards and sloping fields. Enghien and Turenne found it hard to believe that these entrenchments could have been built in a single night. To achieve this, Mercy had organised his men into what we would today call 'three eights': while a third of the men rested and another third kept watch for the French, the last third built the new defences.

Nevertheless, the decision had been taken to attack the new line on Friday morning at the crack of dawn

Mercy described the day of 4 August as:

> From early morning, they [the enemy] recognised our presence and ranged themselves in battle in front of us, right where we had set up camp; but they did not try anything, either because of the heavy rain that was falling or for some other reason, which allowed us to entrench ourselves, as far as was possible in these few hours and in such bad weather. The enemy, who had remained in position all day, pretended to want to start marching to withdraw; but a cavalryman from the Sporck regiment having deserted and passed through his ranks, he stopped short and returned to the old camp. As the prisoners said, this defector announced to the enemy that we had decided to send the baggage forward and withdraw; whereupon the enemy resolved to attack us the following day.[29]

The Bavarian general drew up his regiments on the Josephberg plateau. He put his battalions in two lines between the Josephberg and the Wonnhalde Tower, further south, where 'there are still some ruins of a tower, at the foot of which the highest mountain in the Black Forest begins to rise gradually.'[30] This is where the *Feldmarschall* has stationed 'his largest infantry corps,'[31] perhaps 3,000 men in five or six battalions. 17 artillery pieces faced west, the direction from which the French would arrive, 10 to the north, towards the Josephberg, and 7 to the south, towards the Wonnhalde tower. Dragoons

---

27 The Josephberg is now known as the Lorettoberg, after the small chapel of Notre-Dame de Lorette (Loretto), built in 1657 in memory of the battles of 1644.
28 Bessé, *Relation des Campagnes de Rocroi et Fribourg*, p.107.
29 Duc d'Aumale, *Histoire des princes de Condé pendant les XVIe et XVIIe siècles*, vol. 4, p.605.
30 Bessé, *Relation des Campagnes de Rocroi et Fribourg*, p.107.
31 Ramsay, *Histoire du Vicomte de Turenne, Maréchal-Général des Armées du Roy*, p.129.

THE BATTLE OF FRIBOURG 1644

occupied several redoubts on the slopes. The cavalry was placed on the right wing, between the walls of Fribourg and the wood in front of the village of Wiehre. Part of the infantry was placed in reserve to the east of the mountain.

Bessé summed up the Bavarians' dispositions as:

> The Bavarian camp gave them great advantages, both for defending themselves and for attacking. Their infantry was covered on all sides. One of their wings was supported by the town's cannon and musketry. The other wing was placed on a mountain, whose height alone was sufficient for the safety of the troops occupying it. But they had so many entrenchments to defend that their infantry, weakened by the fatigue of the siege and previous battles, was not enough to guard their camp.[32]

French musketeers c. 1645, contemporary engraving by Jacques Callot. As with the well-known illustrations in *Maréschal de Bataille* (Paris: 1647) these musketeers are somewhat ostentatious in their appearance, especially with the peacock(?) feathers in their hats. This 'extravagance in dress' was commented on by observers at the time and is perhaps an aspect of the French Army that made it stand out from its contemporaries. Note the different lengths of sword blades, indicative that these figures were engraved from life. (Stephen Ede-Borrett collection)

---

32 Bessé, *Relation des Campagnes de Rocroi et Fribourg*, p.110.

7

The Second Battle (5 August 1644)

It rained all night, and at dawn on 5 August, the French army set off on the march. Turenne was in the vanguard that day. His *lieutenant général*, d'Aumont, commanded the infantry. 1,000 musketeers commanded by l'Eschelle (less than 800 according to the *Memoirs of the Maréchal de Turenne*), 1,000 cavalry (eight or ten squadrons according to the *Memoirs of the Maréchal de Turenne*[1]), and 4 artillery pieces under the command of Taupadel were detached to form the extreme right of the army, behind the forest to the south of Wonnhalde. They were ordered to attack on the side of the ruined tower, but not before the rest of the line had been engaged. Enghien wanted all the attacks to be coordinated. L'Eschelle's musketeers were followed by d'Aubeterre and du Tot's brigade led by d'Aumont and by Taupadel's cavalry. The Montausier and Weimarian infantry brigades provided support.

On the left wing, in the plain, Enghien divided the infantry into two columns: d'Espenan commanded the first (Persan and Enghien brigades) and the Count of Tournon the second (Conti and Mazarin brigades). The infantry of the Army of Champagne was ordered to '*double to the left*' - i.e. to deploy on its left[2] - before coming within cannon range. Two companies of gendarmes, led by *Maréchal* Mauvilliers, were to support d'Espenan. On the extreme left, *Maréchal* de Guiche's cavalry, with Palluau and Marsin under his command, provided cover against Jean de Werth's Bavarian cavalry. The artillery, which numbered around 40 pieces, was divided into several batteries under the command of the Marquis de Chouppes.

---

1   Marichal, *Mémoires du Maréchal de Turenne*, p.17.
2   The French army, coming from the west, emerged from the plain in column, then turned right, i.e. south, towards Merzhausen. Turenne's corps was in the vanguard and would hold the right of the army after the regiments had 'doubled to the left,' i.e. pivoted to their left to line up in front of the enemy army. Similarly, the Corps d'Enghien would occupy the centre. The cavalry, as rearguard, would be on the left wing.

THE BATTLE OF FRIBOURG 1644

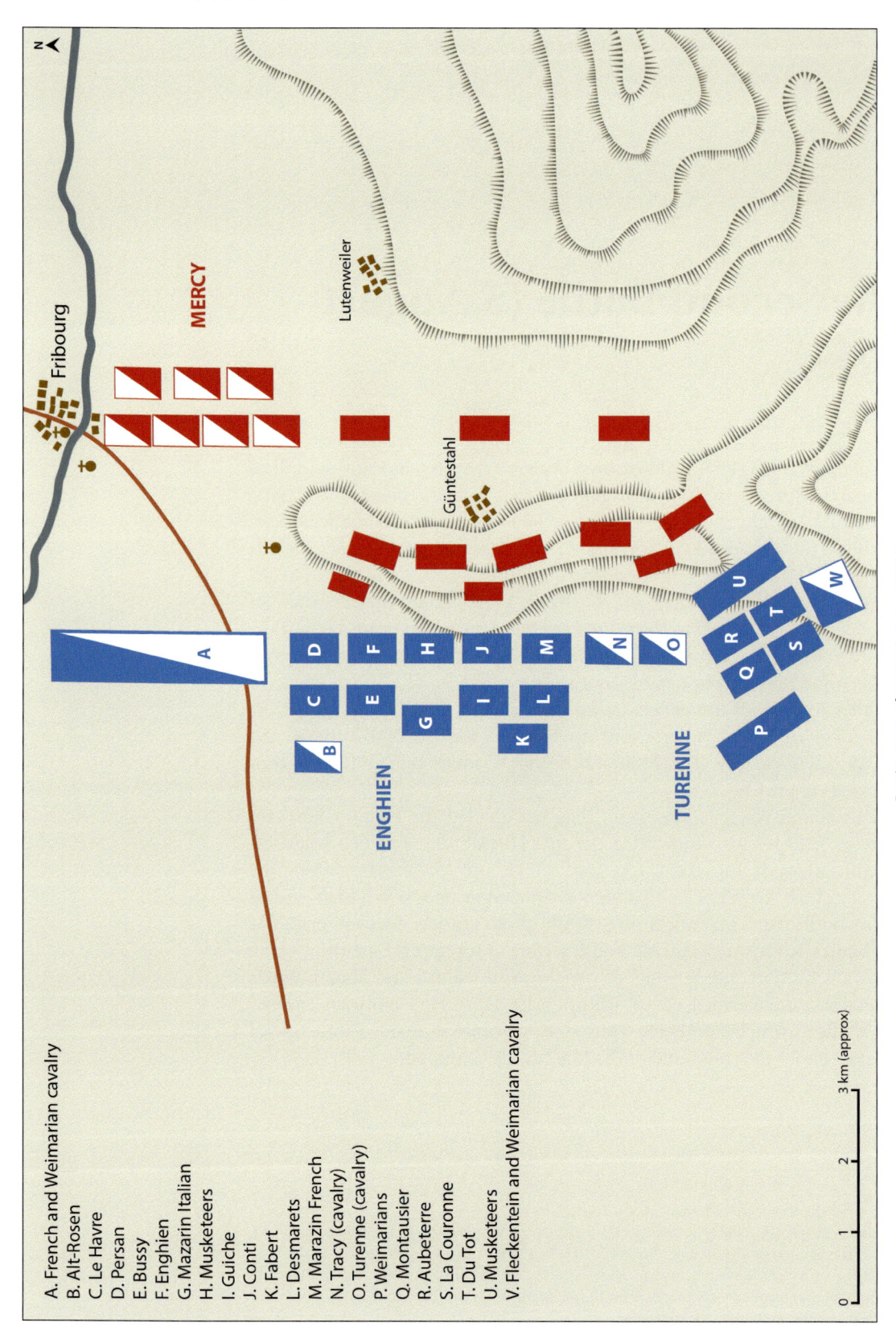

MERCY

Fribourg
Lutenweiler
Güntestahl

ENGHIEN
TURENNE

Deployment of armies 5 August 1644

A. French and Weimarian cavalry
B. Alt-Rosen
C. Le Havre
D. Persan
E. Bussy
F. Enghien
G. Mazarin Italian
H. Musketeers
I. Guiche
J. Conti
K. Fabert
L. Desmarets
M. Marazin French
N. Tracy (cavalry)
O. Turenne (cavalry)
P. Weimarians
Q. Montausier
R. Aubeterre
S. La Couronne
T. Du Tot
U. Musketeers
V. Fleckentein and Weimarian cavalry

0 1 2 3 km (approx)

THE SECOND BATTLE (5 AUGUST 1644)

While the rearguard deployed, awaiting the signal, l'Eschelle fired the few guns at his disposal. To comply with the Duc d'Enghien's orders, he had to hear the sound of the musketry because, separated from the main columns by woods and tall trees, he could not see them. But that day, things did not go according to plan. De Chouppes wrote:

> Through a misunderstanding, the battle began where it was not supposed to begin: those who were supposed to attack first did not do so; and those who were not supposed to attack, did so where it was not necessary, with the result that we were repulsed with many casualties.[3]

The *Gazette* reported that:

> some of our men advanced against the orders they had been given not to engage in anything, and attacked a redoubt that the enemies had at the foot of the hill, which they abandoned; but they made such a great discharge from above that it made those at the head of the right-hand attack believe that it was the signal to give everywhere.[4]

What happened? Early in the morning, following a reconnaissance, an officer from the Fleckenstein cavalry regiment came to warn Turenne that the Bavarians seemed to be in great confusion and had removed their baggage. The *Maréchal* immediately informed the Duc d'Enghien. After ordering the army to wait for their return before launching an attack, the two men set off to find out for themselves what had happened.[5] They covered around 2,000 paces. If Bessé is to be believed, La Moussaye believes that their aim was to 'discover the rear of the enemy's army and see their order of battle.'[6]

It was 8 o'clock. D'Espenan, having spotted an advanced enemy redoubt, sent 'a few musketeers to seize it, without waiting for orders from *M. le* Duc, or *M. le Maréchal* de Grammont (i.e. de Guiche); thinking, as I believe, that the matter would not have such a great outcome, or perhaps also to show himself off by some small action.'[7] La Moussaye is less severe with d'Espenan, he thought that d'Espenan 'detached a few men with the intention of making a false attack on a small redoubt which was on his way to the Bavarians. Although at first he sent very few men, the fight gradually broke out on both sides; the enemies supported those who were defending their redoubt; Espenan reinforced those who were attacking.'[8]

Having chased off a few dragoons, d'Espenan ordered the attack to continue as far as the enemy lines. Small cause, big effect: the Bavarians reacted to this attack by opening fire on the French infantry, sowing death among the attackers. De Guiche recounted the attack as follows:

---

3 Chouppes, *Mémoires du Marquis de Chouppes, Lieutenant Général des Armées du Roi*, p.73.
4 Renaudot, *Recueil des Gazettes et Nouvelles Ordinaires et Extraordinaires et autres relations des choses avenues toute l'année mille six cents quarante-quatre*, p.667.
5 Marichal, *Mémoires du Maréchal de Turenne*, p.18.
6 Bessé, *Relation des Campagnes de Rocroi et Fribourg*, p.111.
7 Marichal, *Mémoires du Maréchal de Turenne*, p.19.
8 Bessé, *Relation des Campagnes de Rocroi et Fribourg*, pp.111–112.

> Sieur d'Espenan, having first taken a redoubt that a few dragoons were guarding and which was at the bottom of the enemy position, had such high hopes that he thought all he had to do was march up and defeat them; but he was very much mistaken, for they always held their ground with unrivalled firmness and without it ever being possible to breach them. It was there that a large number of soldiers and officers were killed, as well as the two *sergents de bataille*.[9]

From the right wing, l'Eschelle and Taupadel could not see the operations: they therefore had to engage only at the sound of the musketry. Passing in front of his troops, Turenne is said to have expressly told them 'not to move from their posts, and that he would return immediately.'[10] Ramsay is equally categorical, stating that the Duke and Vicomte 'forbade the officers to undertake anything in their absence.'[11] However, having heard the enemy salvo, Taupadel's vanguard moved off and marched towards the enemy. The *Gazette Renaudot* endeavours to explain this action, reporting that l'Eschelle, 'seeing our people in combat, thought he should support them with the thousand musketeers he commanded, and had them supported by the Aubeterre and Tot regiments.'[12]

D'Aumont, placed in support, immediately ordered his brigade (Aubeterre and du Tot) to march into battle. His men approached the slopes of the mountain, crossed some wooded areas and advanced towards the entrenchments held by the Bavarian army. Mercy had had time to observe these movements: his battalions had no trouble repelling this poorly coordinated attack. The *Gazette Renaudot* explains that 'the enemies regained heart and refreshed the rest of their troops who were not entertained elsewhere, because our other attacks could not be ready, this one having been precipitated.'[13]

At the sound of the fighting, Enghien and Turenne rushed back but could only see the extent of the disaster. The right wing was in disarray: l'Eschelle had been killed at the head of his men, and his musketeers, beaten, withdrew. Taupadel did the same with the cavalry. Most of the officers were dead or wounded and two of the cannon had been dismantled. Only Fleckenstein's cavalry regiment remained under fire from the infantry so steadfastly that it 'lost half its men.'[14] Faced with this threat, the Bavarians, who had begun the pursuit, cautiously preferred to withdraw to their posts. De Chouppes, in charge of the artillery, arrived on the scene after the action. He said that several officers had suffered the same fate as l'Eschelle and that 'there were many wounded. Those in command of the battery were no happier. Several were killed; the commander had his arm broken; and two pieces of cannon

---

9   Gramont, *Mémoires du Maréchal de Gramont*, tome 7, p.257.
10 Marichal, *Mémoires du Maréchal de Turenne*, p.19.
11 Ramsay, *Histoire du Vicomte de Turenne, Maréchal-Général des Armées du Roy*, p.130.
12 Renaudot, *Recueil des Gazettes et Nouvelles Ordinaires et Extraordinaires et autres relations des choses avenues toute l'année mille six cents quarante-quatre*, p.667.
13 Renaudot, *Recueil des Gazettes et Nouvelles Ordinaires et Extraordinaires et autres relations des choses avenues toute l'année mille six cents quarante-quatre*, p.668.
14 Marichal, *Mémoires du Maréchal de Turenne*, p.20.

THE SECOND BATTLE (5 AUGUST 1644)

had been dismounted. I decided to stay in this place to try and remedy the mess.'[15]

Enghien resigned himself to stopping the attack. He often exposed himself to Bavarian fire: the pommel of his saddle was blown off by a cannonball and the scabbard of his sword was shattered by a musket shot.[16] The Comte de Guiche had a horse killed beneath him. Taking advantage of this respite, Turenne moved towards the rest of his infantry, 3,000 men who had not yet been engaged. Enghien joined d'Espenan, whose infantry had been pushed back, and set about putting his lines in order. While the French battalions were brought back out of musket range, the Duc prepared a new attack: 'We stayed in this position for a long time, because it takes a lot to order an attack in difficult places that are not easy to see from one another.'[17]

Enghien was not discouraged: he wanted to continue the attack, but by concentrating his attack on the abattis. He reorganised his battalions into two corps: Persan, Conti, Le Havre and Bussy on the left, Enghien, Mazarin-Français, Guiche, Desmarets and Fabert on the right. In front of this line of battalions, Mauvilliers, *sergent de bataille*, commanded 400 detached musketeers. D'Aumont, with the regiments that had just fought, led by the Aubeterre brigade, was to provide a diversion on the right wing. Turenne had assured Enghien that he would hold out until nightfall whatever the outcome of this offensive. Finally, the cavalry had to support the wings: the *gendarmes* and the squadrons of *chevau-légers* commanded by Palluau on the left, the regiments of Tracy and Turenne on the right of the brigades of the French army. The Mazarin-Italian infantry regiment and the Alt-Rosen cavalry regiment were in reserve. The Compte de Guiche's cavalry faced the Bavarian cavalry.[18] De Guiche 'had to attack from the flank or support with cavalry, if the attack had been somewhat successful.'[19] The Weimarian cavalry regiments supported the army on the extreme right.

It was probably 3p.m. The battalions advanced in this order as far as a wooded ridge held by both the Bavarian infantry and the Bavarian cavalry, who had dismounted: 'Our troops marched in this order as far as a wooded ridge that the enemies had made, and behind which they had taken up their position with most of their cavalry, some of which had dismounted.'[20] Mauvilliers' musketeers led the assault. The attack was carried out vigorously, but the French ardour was hampered by obstacles. According to Bessé, 'no sooner had the first men of this new attack entered the wood than the Bavarians fired an extraordinary salvo.'[21] This salvo did not dampen the

---

15 Chouppes, *Mémoires du Marquis de Chouppes, Lieutenant Général des Armées du Roi,* p.77.
16 Bessé, *Relation des campagnes de Rocroi et Fribourg,* p.114; De Chouppes, *Mémoires du Marquis de Chouppes,* p.78; Renaudot, *Recueil des Gazettes et Nouvelles Ordinaires et Extraordinaires et autres relations des choses avenues toute l'année mille six cents quarante-quatre,* p.669.
17 Marichal, *Mémoires du Maréchal de Turenne,* p.20.
18 Renaudot, *Recueil des Gazettes et Nouvelles Ordinaires et Extraordinaires et autres relations des choses avenues toute l'année mille six cents quarante-quatre,* p.669.
19 Marichal, *Mémoires du Maréchal de Turenne,* p.20.
20 Renaudot, *Recueil des Gazettes et Nouvelles Ordinaires et Extraordinaires et autres relations des choses avenues toute l'année mille six cents quarante-quatre,* p.669.
21 Bessé, *Relation des Campagnes de Rocroi et Fribourg,* in Collection de Petits Classiques François, p.115.

THE BATTLE OF FRIBOURG 1644

Weimarian horse and foot, watercolour by K. A. Wilke. (Bibliothèque Universitaire de Lausanne, photo by the author)

resolve of the French, who 'marched against them in very good order to try and force this entrenchment of trees.'[22]

While d'Enghien was asking de Chouppes to reposition the guns, he learned that Mauvilliers had been killed. He sent the Marquis de Castelnau-Mauvissière to replace him and to rally the musketeers. However, although Castelnau-Mauvissière 'did his duty as a man of courage and fought with great valour until nightfall,'[23] he was unable to break through the Bavarian lines. Enghien led on the Mazarin-Français regiment, which had remained in reserve until then; however, the attack was finally repulsed.

Generalmajor Gaspar de Mercy had to dismount to support his dismounted cavalry after it had been driven from its entrenchments. It was now the turn of the French to be pushed back. Neither side wanted to give up. Once again,

> both sides fired so furiously that the noise and smoke confused everything and they could only recognise each other by the flash of the artillery fire and musket fire. All the surrounding woods resounded with a frightful roar, adding to the horror of the battle. The soldiers were so relentless, some forcing the entrenchments, others defending them, that if it hadn't been for the night, there would have been the greatest carnage on both sides.[24]

Gaspar de Mercy was killed in this action.

On the right wing, Turenne's infantry, which was already very weak, seemed to attack with less conviction. The d'Aubeterre brigade was unable to break through the enemy positions: Turenne supported it with the la Couronne brigade.[25] During both phases of the battle, the Tot and la Couronne regiments suffered particularly badly, losing 16 officers and 200 soldiers in the fighting. Fleckenstein's cavalry, supporting d'Aumont, once again showed admirable courage, leaving half of their number on the battlefield.

Generals and officers struggled, pressing and threatening their soldiers. Even the French cavalry fired shots that day: the *gendarmerie*, placed as it should be in support of the infantry, carried out 'a very fine action.'[26] La Boulaye in command of these elite companies led his men to the enemy entrenchments, had them cock their pistols and began the skirmish. Cavalry from the Turenne and Tracy regiments also went on the attack, some mounted, others on foot. Clisson, a cornet in the Tracy regiment, even managed to plant his standard on the parapet before being killed.

Maréchal de Guiche was worried about the situation. If his memoirs are to be believed, after leaving his wing he found the infantry 'in appalling disarray, doing nothing more than parrying their bellies against the musketry, which they tried to protect by sticking as hard as they could against the trees that

---

22 Bessé, *Relation des Campagnes de Rocroi et Fribourg*, p.115.
23 Chouppes, *Mémoires du Marquis de Chouppes, Lieutenant Général des Armées du Roi*, pp.78–79.
24 Bessé, *Relation des Campagnes de Rocroi et Fribourg*, p.116.
25 Renaudot, *Recueil des Gazettes et Nouvelles Ordinaires et Extraordinaires et autres relations des choses avenues toute l'année mille six cents quarante-quatre*, p.669.
26 Bessé, *Relation des Campagnes de Rocroi et Fribourg*, in Collection de Petits Classiques François, p.116.

the enemies had made.'[27] He then joined Enghien and Turenne and painted a picture of exhausted infantry. Enghien agreed but feared that withdrawing before nightfall would leave the army at the mercy of enemy cavalry. De Guiche reassured him by arguing that he would take care of this, 'in such a way that they would not dare to bite.'[28] According to De Chouppes, it was the Duc d'Enghien who sent for Turenne and de Guiche, as well as himself, to discuss the situation:

French *gendarmes*, watercolour by K. A. Wilke. (Bibliothèque Universitaire de Lausanne, photo by the author)

After carefully considering the state of affairs and especially the great loss of men that we had just suffered, including a very large number of officers, we all agreed that there was no other course for us to take than to withdraw. The difficulty was to do so. We were as close as we could get to the enemy; we had eight or ten dismounted cannon; we had to put them on new mountings or abandon them.[29]

Enghien could not bring himself to abandon them. De Chouppes had trumpets and drums sound to cover the noise of the cannons being mounted, while Rosen and Taupadel brought him the horses and arms he needed: 500 cavalrymen dismounted to handle the guns and 4,000 horses were made available to move them.

The fighting lasted six hours. French losses were enormous, Turenne wrote in his memoirs: 'the infantry was almost completely ruined …. a very large number of officers were killed; *M.* de l'Echelle and *M.* de Mauvilliers, *sergents de battaile*, and almost all the corps commanders and some of the infantry officers [were casualties].'[30] The Persan, Enghien and Conti infantry regiments seem to have

---

27 Gramont, *Mémoires du Maréchal de Gramont*, tome 7, p.258.
28 Gramont, *Mémoires du Maréchal de Gramont*, tome 7, p.258.
29 Chouppes, *Mémoires du Marquis de Chouppes, Lieutenant Général des Armées du Roi*, p.79.
30 Marichal, *Mémoires du Maréchal de Turenne*, pp.21–22.

THE SECOND BATTLE (5 AUGUST 1644)

suffered particularly badly. The Tracy cavalry regiment also left many dead on the battlefield.

Bavarian losses were just as heavy, with the infantry strength almost halved since the first day. The Hasslang and Holz regiments and 300 musketeers were annihilated on the first day. The Winterscheid regiment also seems to have suffered greatly. A further 700 to 800 casualties were reported during the second attack.[31] Ramsay estimates that the Bavarians lost half their infantry on 3 August – which is excessive, as we have seen – and 1,200 men on 5 August.[32] Mercy particularly deplored the loss of his brother Gaspard, the army's *Generalmajor*.

In a letter dated 7 August, Mercy explained that the French had attacked them because they believed that, having decided to withdraw, the Bavarians were on the march:

French fifer, drummer and officer, watercolour by K. A. Wilke. (Bibliothèque Universitaire de Lausanne, photo by the author)

---

31 Renaudot, *Recueil des Gazettes et Nouvelles Ordinaires et Extraordinaires et autres relations des choses avenues toute l'année mille six cents quarante-quatre*, p.669.
32 Ramsay, *Histoire du Vicomte de Turenne, Maréchal-Général des Armées du Roy*, p.131.

But although he attacked us on several occasions, and even until nightfall, with the usual fury that he shows in this war, he found such resistance that he lost a *maréchal de camp* and a good number of colonels and officers killed. He will certainly not try anything against us any time soon on this ground; and if the cavalry had not been much superior to ours, a general action would have been engaged, which would have enabled us, I believe, to destroy him. During the night [of 5 to 6 August], the enemy withdrew in silence and returned to his camp; he is still there today; he left a host of dead on the ground. Due to a lack of cavalry, we had to stop. According to reports from all the prisoners, the enemy's losses amounted to several thousand dead and wounded. We too suffered and lost several hundred men, but the main damage and the greatest loss consisted in the death of a faithful servant of the Prince-Elector, my brother the *general wachtmeister*, in that of *Colonel* Miehr, and in the disabling of many officers. The enemy has remained in the position he has taken, that is to say in our old camp, and we are facing him. Last night [the evening of 6 August], he also began to dig in; but today, at 4 a.m., we sounded the alarm in his camp. We are digging in as well as we can, although we are short of food. We are already forced to look for them at a distance of 6, 7 or 8 hours. The enemy can't stay here any longer than we can, because of the same lack of food.[33]

That same day, the Bavarian general wrote:

It is said that the enemy still has 5,000 infantry and cavalry. He will not be able to force me into this position, but he will be able to take control of the countryside. If I still had 2,000 cavalry and as many infantry, I would hope, with God's help, to make him cross the Rhine again. I hope that my master will soon bring up our dismounted cavalry. But there is no remedy for the infantry.[34]

From 6 to 10 August

Saturday was a day of rest, and the wounded were taken to Brisach on carts and stretchers, Enghien also had the artillery taken there. The Comte de Guiche stated that they

stayed in the camp for three days, which were used to bring back to Brisach, by some of the army carts, all the officers and soldiers who had been wounded in these two great actions. It was a terrible stay, because they stayed among all the dead bodies, which caused such an infection that many people died: but there was no way of doing otherwise, and the disease was inevitable.[35]

Once these arrangements had been made, Enghien convened a new council of war. It was decided to bypass the enemy via Langen Denzlingen and the

---

33 Duc d'Aumale, *Histoire des princes de Condé pendant les XVIe et XVIIe siècles*, vol. 4, pp.606–608.
34 Duc d'Aumale, *Histoire des princes de Condé pendant les XVIe et XVIIe siècles*, vol. 4, pp.606–608.
35 Gramont, *Mémoires du Maréchal de Gramont*, tome 7, p.258.

THE SECOND BATTLE (5 AUGUST 1644)

Saint-Pierre valley, as d'Erlach had suggested a few days earlier. In a letter written on 8 August, Enghien informed Cardinal Mazarin of his plans:

> The enemy is suffering immensely and I hope that, with God's help, we will either ruin them or at least force them to abandon Fribourg to us. Tomorrow we are marching towards Württemberg in the valley of Langen Denzlingen, which is a post where we will find abundant fodder, from which we can easily draw our supplies from Brisach, from which we will greatly inconvenience the enemies by always holding their rear with strong parties of cavalry, and from which we will be in a position to descend the Rhine whenever we wish, and to take any action we please on that side.[36]

On the morning of 9 August, *Général* Rosen and the Marquis de Castelnau-Mauvissière were sent forward to seize the passage of Saint-Pierre. D'Enghien, Turenne and de Guiche followed at a two-hour march behind with the rest of the army, taking the direction of Langen Denzlingen. 'This march was a little bold,'[37] de Guiche commented in his memoirs, as the French had to expose their flank to the Bavarians. The skilful Mercy, guessing the French intentions, also decided to march towards Württemberg via Glottertal and the Val Saint-Pierre, having left a garrison behind in Fribourg. The dragoon and cuirassier regiments under Gayling formed his vanguard, followed by Ruischenberg's infantry, Jean de Werth and three regiments of mounted harquebusiers forming the rearguard.

On the French side, Rosen advanced at the front, with eight squadrons[38] of 700 to 800 men in total.[39] The Weimarian cavalry had not been much weakened by the previous fighting. In his letter to Mazarin dated 8 August, Enghien stated that 'the German army's cavalry is in the best condition in the world and is certainly infinitely better than last year; they have used the money given to them very well.'[40]

Rosen left around midnight, three or four hours before the rest of the army. Ramsay specifies, 'as he was a very good and experienced officer, he was ordered either to attack some troops that the enemy had separated for the ease of his march, or to stop the main body of the army by harassing it, and thereby give the King's army time to advance.'[41] The country was very rugged. Rosen was followed by Castenau, at the head of 1,000 musketeers, and then by the rest of the army. Behind the Weimarians, the progress of Turenne and Enghien's troops became increasingly difficult. The horsemen often had to dismount or ride in single file. After five or six hours' marching, the royal army reached a small height.

From this position, by the light of dawn[42] Turenne could see his vanguard. Rosen's squadrons were advancing down the valley, 800 metres below. Above

---

36 Duc d'Aumale, *Histoire des princes de Condé pendant les XVIe et XVIIe siècles*, vol. 4, pp.610–611.
37 Gramont, *Mémoires du Maréchal de Gramont*, tome 7, p.258.
38 Marichal, *Mémoires du Maréchal de Turenne*, p.22.
39 Ramsay, *Histoire du Vicomte de Turenne, Maréchal-Général des Armées du Roy*, p.23.
40 Duc d'Aumale, *Histoire des princes de Condé pendant les XVIe et XVIIe siècles*, vol. 4, p.611.
41 Marichal, *Mémoires du Maréchal de Turenne*, p.22.
42 10 August 1644.

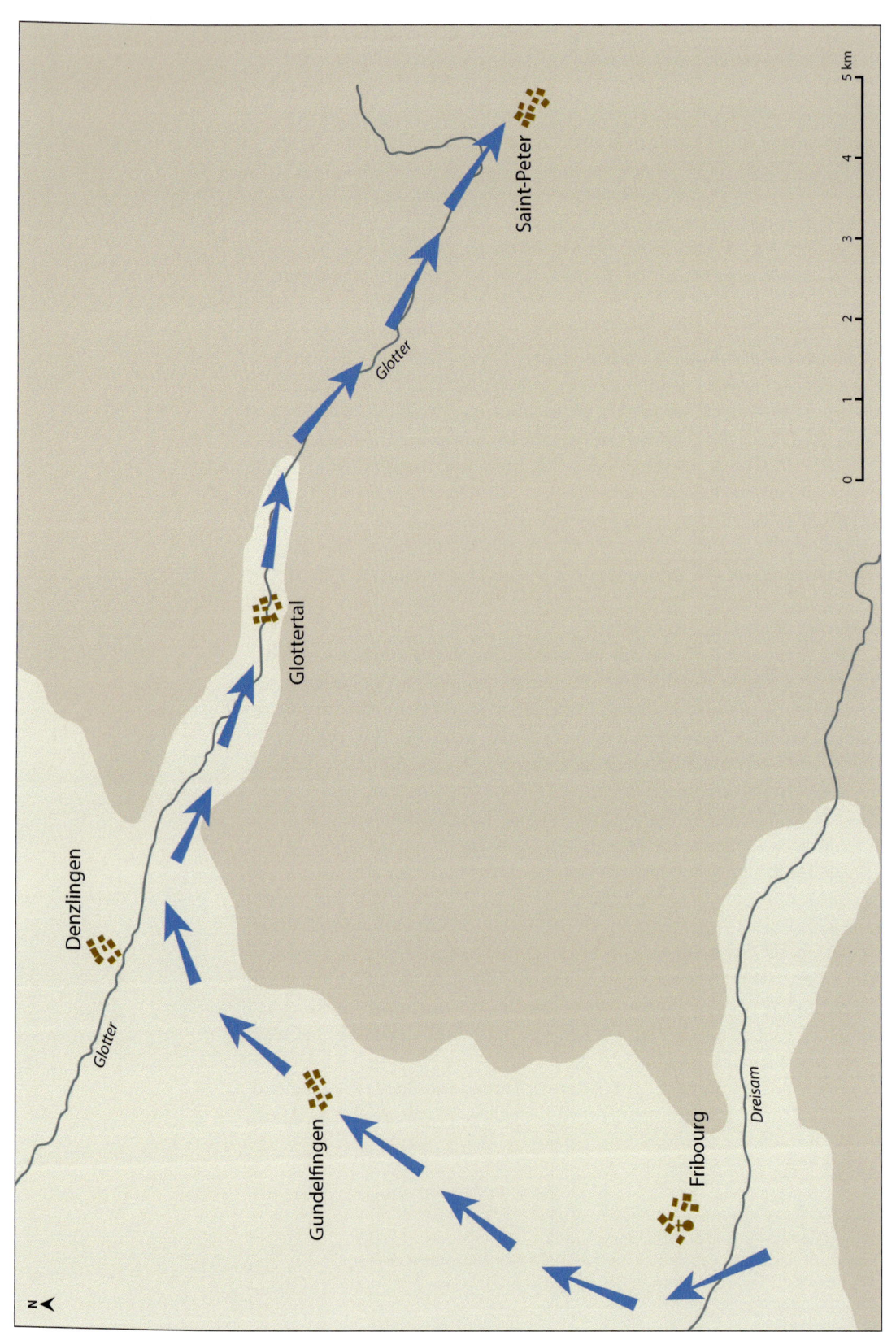

THE BATTLE OF FRIBOURG 1644

Planned movement from 9 to 10 August 1644.

THE SECOND BATTLE (5 AUGUST 1644)

them, on Mont Saint-Pierre, Mercy's army was withdrawing. Rosen could only see their rearguard as he approached the mountain close on their heels. On the orders of the Duc d'Enghien, Turenne sent a messenger to warn him of the situation. He was already within musket range of the enemy army and the first shots were fired.

Rosen, watercolour by K. A. Wilke. (Bibliothèque Universitaire de Lausanne, photo by the author)

Mercy quickly assessed the situation. To get out of the valley, he would have to force his way through Rosen, with baggage and artillery, while the entire French army was now in sight. He therefore decided to continue his retreat. After abandoning his wagons, artillery and baggage, he led his troops through the Abbey of Saint-Pierre, which overlooked the valley. He spotted the Weimarian horsemen emerging from the road and forming up into squadrons. Mercy reacted swiftly, charging Rosen's vanguard, taking several of his

THE BATTLE OF FRIBOURG 1644

Cavalry Combat, engraving by Stefano Della Bella, from Thomas Dodd, *A Collection of Etchings by that Inimitable Artist Stefano Della Bella* (London: H.R. Young, 1818). (Public Domain)

standards and 'beating him with his back to his belly.'[43] Turenne, who was more measured, presented the affair differently: 'some enemy squadrons having wanted to advance in front of their infantry. *Mr* Rosen's cavalry drove them back, and following them in order, three or four battalions discharged on him, which stopped the cavalry without nevertheless causing confusion.'[44] The Weimarian squadrons were now deployed in two lines, stoically enduring the enemy fire. Outnumbered, Rosen decided to withdraw in order, although he had lost four or five standards. According to Turenne, the Bavarian cavalry

> did not dare to push them vigorously for fear of moving too far away from their infantry; or else because, still surprised by the fighting of the previous days, their main intention was to withdraw without combat. These first squadrons of Rosen having been supported by those of the second line, and the whole body of the enemy cavalry and infantry continuing to march against them and being forty or fifty paces from each other, they withdrew about five or six hundred paces mingled with the enemy, who made more use of the fire of their infantry than of their cavalry.[45]

In reality, Gayling's cuirassiers refused to pursue the Weimarian squadrons, and the *Feldmarschall* was furious.

Mercy's main aim was to cover his own retreat. He could already see two French squadrons on the hill from which Turenne was watching. Judging that it was time to withdraw, he resumed his march towards Villingen.[46] Rosen ordered his squadrons to halt, as they were no longer in a position to pursue the enemy. While Mercy resumed its march through the woods towards Württemberg, the French, hot and two hours behind schedule, cautiously resumed the pursuit, but they soon gave up. The army was ordered to camp at the Abbey of Saint-Pierre, where the soldiers would have the satisfaction of

---

43   Gramont, *Mémoires du Maréchal de Gramont,* tome 7, p.258.
44   Marichal, *Mémoires du Maréchal de Turenne*, p.24.
45   Marichal, *Mémoires du Maréchal de Turenne*, p.24.
46   Villingen-Schwenningen, a town further east, in the south-west of Baden-Württemberg.

THE SECOND BATTLE (5 AUGUST 1644)

Baggage train, engraving by Stefano Della Bella, from Thomas Dodd, *A Collection of Etchings by that Inimitable Artist Stefano Della Bella* (London: H.R. Young, 1818). (Public Domain)

looting the Bavarian baggage that was in their hands. On 11 August, Enghien led the exhausted army back to Denzlingen. At the same time, Mercy brought the Bavarian army back to Schömberg.

8

Epilogue

Enghien would have liked to retake Fribourg, but Turenne dissuaded him. Even weakened, it would have taken a major effort to take the town, and Turenne thought that the opportunity to take control of the entire course of the Rhine was too good to pass up. For the time being, Mazarin asked Turenne to see to it that the army in Germany was reformed, 'to gain stable quarters for it, so that it is not obliged to keep running as it has done up until now in search of.'[1] The Cardinal was counting on the return of Torstensson following his campaign in Denmark and the support of the Landgraf von Hesse before resuming his efforts in Germany.

On 8 August, the Duc d'Enghien wrote to his father:

> in the two battles I fought near Fribourg with the Bavarian army, the enemy army ran the risk of being completely defeated, but at least it was extremely ruined. As far as I am concerned, I lost many officers, including poor Mauvilly who was killed. This is certainly the greatest loss we could have made. .... I have lost many horses and almost all my people have been wounded.[2]

In the letter of the same day to Mazarin, he added:

> I will say nothing about *Mr Maréchal* de Guiche, he is too well known to you for me to need to tell you anything about him. All I can say is that on this occasion he has surpassed, if he can, your expectations. *Mr Maréchal* de Turenne served with all the heart and ability imaginable. *Messieurs* d'Espenan, de Palluau, d'Aumont, de Tournon and de Marsin worked wonders.... Leschelle was wounded very dangerously after having served very usefully, and one cannot believe what honour poor Mauvilly had acquired when he died. All our troops did their duty very well and I swear to you that never has an army been so close to losing its battle as the enemy. God did not want it. We may have the opportunity again. Your infantry regiment did everything that could be expected of it, but especially the Marquis de Castelnau stood out to the last degree; I believe that, at this hour when we no longer have a *sergent de bataille*, you must send him the letter to

---

1   Chéruel, *Lettres du Cardinal Mazarin pendant son ministère,* vol.1, pp.36–37.
2   Duc d'Aumale, *Histoire des Princes de Condé pendant les XVIe et XVIIe siècles,* vol. 4, pp.608–609.

serve. He will do it very well and he deserves more than that, if I dare say so. My regiments did wonderfully and I lost a very large number of officers. But Chamilly, my lieutenant colonel, and Saint Point, Conti's first captain, worked miracles. The Persan regiment stood out, but it lost poor La Freysinette. I beg you to grant the lieutenant colonelcy to Du Bout-du-Bois, who is its first captain. He has served with great dignity, and if, in addition, the position is his by right.[3]

The losses on both sides were enormous. The French lost more than 7,000 men, and the Bavarians nearly 3,000, including almost 2,000 on the first day. Varillas in *Politique de la Maison d'Autriche,* describes Mazarin's reaction when he heard the news as follows:

> The fatal day of Fribourg brought tears to his eyes, and his great courage was overwhelmed with grief when he learned that they had persisted in making themselves masters of an almost inaccessible post or camp, which had caused so much bloodshed and so many honest people to leave, that history pities them, and it is impossible to read the account of this disastrous victory without horror. We can say that we were done for, and France would have been lost if it had taken many like it with it. Cadméenne was not so cruel, and the loss of this bloody and unfortunate battle, and the retreat of our army would have been much more useful and advantageous to our affairs, than the success.[4]

The King was nonetheless pleased, as this letter testifies:

> Our dearest and most loyal friends, since the day of Fribourg, our dearest and most beloved cousin the Duc d'Enghien has continued to use our armies so happily that in less than three weeks he has made himself master of Philipsbourg, even though it is one of the most important places in Germany, both for its base and for its fortress. He is even said to have caused such terror in all these countries that the people of Speyer voluntarily surrendered to our authority a few days ago. And we have noticed that several other considerable towns are on the point of following this example, and of avoiding by voluntary obedience the evils of which they are threatened, if they are forced to do so by force. For this reason, we feel obliged to render to God the gratitude that is due to Him.[5]

---

3   Duc d'Aumale, *Histoire des Princes de Condé pendant les XVIe et XVIIe siècles*, vol. 4, pp.609–610.
4   Antoine Varillas, *La politique de la Maison d'Autriche* (Paris: Antoine Sommaville, 1658), p.30.
5   Aimé Champollion-Figeac (ed.), *Mémoires de Mathieu Molé,* (Paris: Librarie de l'Histoire de France, 1856), time 3, p.112.

THE BATTLE OF FRIBOURG 1644

Crippled, *The Miseries and Misfortunes of War*, engraving by Jacques Callot. (Public domain)

Conclusion

During these seven days, Mercy demonstrated exceptional tactical skills. In the end, he managed to keep his army operational. Although Enghien's relentlessness seemed questionable, his behaviour was worthy of admiration: his prompt decisions, tenacity and energy on the battlefield were decisive and enabled him to avoid a fatal outcome.

Almost two centuries later, Napoleon condemned the choices made by the Duc d'Enghien during the Battle of Fribourg: 'The Prince of Condé has violated one of the principles of mountain warfare: never attack troops occupying good positions in the mountains, but flush them out by occupying camps on their flanks or their rear.'[1] With a little hindsight, this judgement is harsh. When Turenne called on Enghien to help, Fribourg, although under siege, was still in French hands. The opportunity to catch the Bavarians in the crossfire was too good. And that is exactly what Turenne said in a letter he wrote to Enghien on 26 July: 'as it is impossible for the enemy to withdraw in the way they have engaged below the mountains.'[2] The Duc had reacted quickly, but he was still too late. Fribourg capitulated on 28 July, three days before he arrived in Brisach.

D'Erlach's proposal to bypass the enemy position via the Val Saint-Pierre seemed attractive. Such a strategy could have helped to take the Bavarian Army from the rear and, above all, to cut it off from its supply bases. However, it would have meant marching in front of Mercy's lines, through woods and marshes. Such a manoeuvre would inevitably have been discovered by the Bavarian general's sagacity, and this would have meant taking the risk of giving the initiative back to the Bavarians. What's more, if it had succeeded, this manoeuvre would have left the Bavarians no way out. The battle would then have been hopeless because, as Sun Tzu says, you should never push 'a desperate enemy.' It is better to 'leave a way out for a surrounded enemy' than to risk a fatal battle.[3]

After the retreat of the Bavarians, Turenne was right to convince the Duc d'Enghien not to retake Fribourg. On 23 August, the two men headed back north to Phillipsburg. The town fell on 12 September. Then it was the turn of Worms, Oppenheim, Mainz, Landau, Mannheim and Neustadt. By the end

---

1 Napoléon Bonaparte, *Précis des Guerres du Maréchal de Turenne*, p.119.
2 Duc d'Aumale, *Histoire des Princes de Condé pendant les XVIe et XVIIe siècles*, vol. 4, p.602.
3 Sun Tzu, *The Art of War*, translated by Samuel B. Griffith (Oxford: Oxford University Press, 1963), pp.147–148.

THE BATTLE OF FRIBOURG 1644

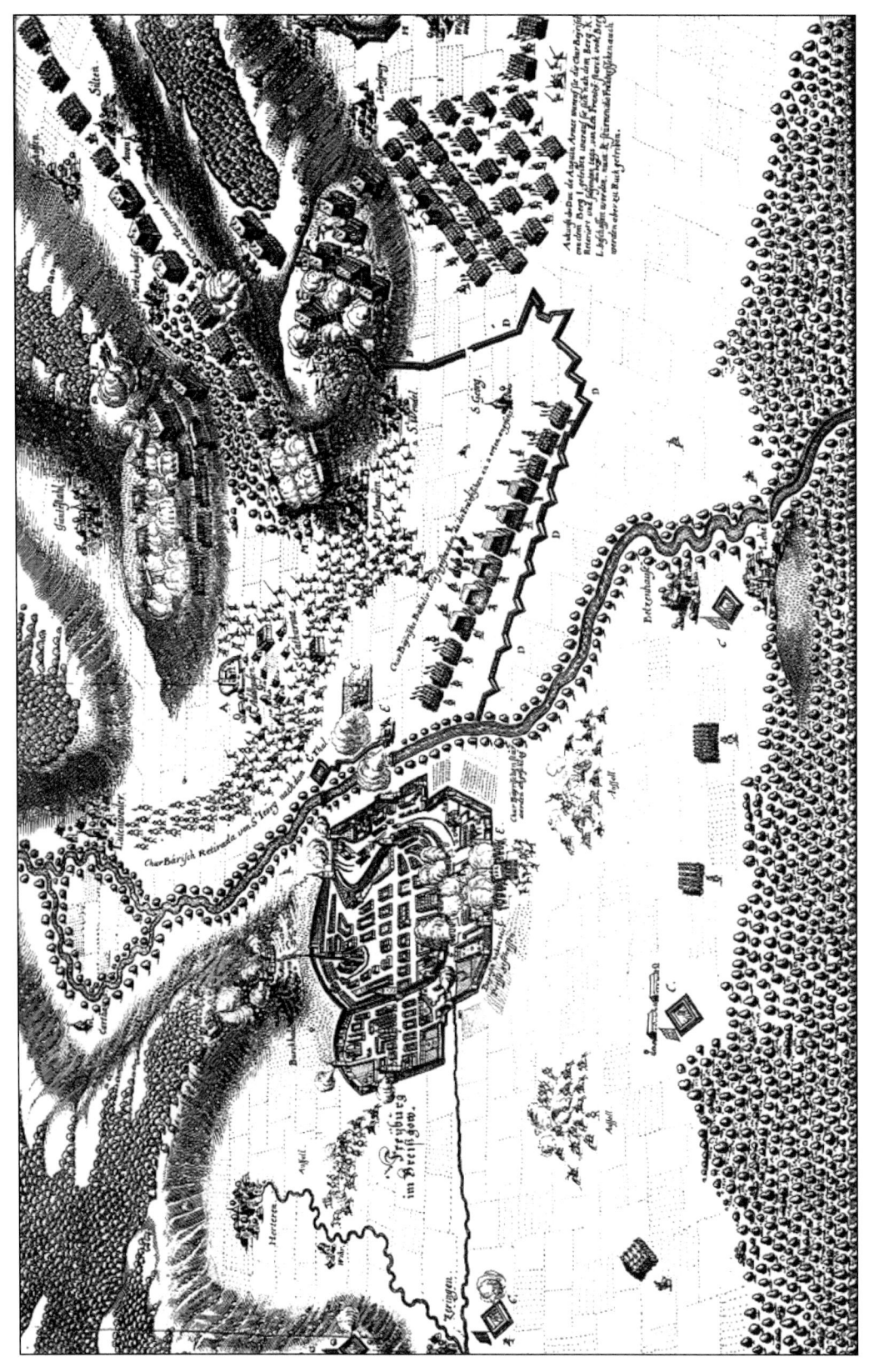

First Battle of Fribourg, map from *Theatrum Europaeum*. (Public domain)

CONCLUSION

of October 1644, the French were in control of the Palatinate and the entire course of the Rhine between Strasbourg and Coblenz. This strategic choice illustrates another of the principles theorised by the Chinese strategist: 'what is essential in war is victory, not prolonged operations.'[4]

The Battle of Freibourg, along with the Battle of Alerheim (or the second Nördlingen), which took place exactly one year later on 3 August 1645 and saw the same protagonists, Enghien and Condé against Mercy, contribute to shaping the genius of two of France's greatest generals: the future Grand Condé and Turenne.

Although the Duc d'Enghien encountered a few more difficulties in the years that followed (as at the Siege of Lérida in 1647), two years later he fought the Battle of Lens on 20 August 1648, which can be considered one of his masterpieces. The experiences of Fribourg, Alerheim and Llerida, battles in which Condé exhausted his forces in frontal assaults, probably helped to show him that energy and speed of decision were not enough to win. Armed with this knowledge, and with his army facing the solid positions of Erzherzog Leopold's army established between Lens and Liévin, Condé feigned a retreat towards Béthune. And the ruse worked. Beck let himself be fooled and succeeded in convincing Erzherzog Leopold to leave his good positions and set off in pursuit of the French. Early in the morning, as his army crested a valley, he saw the French army facing him. It was a manoeuvre that Napoleon would repeat at Austerlitz. 'The whole art of war is based on deception' wrote Sun Tzu, 'which is why, when you are capable, feign incapacity; when you are active, passivity. (…) Bait the enemy to ensnare him; simulate disorder and strike him.'[5]

As for Turenne, it was the campaign of 1646, two years later, that would reveal his genius. This little-known campaign will remain one of the finest examples of indirect style in military history. At the beginning of 1646, the peace negotiations were delicate: The French and Swedes, allies since 1635, did not trust each other. Their Imperial and Bavarian opponents were no more united. On the French side, Vicomte de Turenne was the only one who could get along with the Swedes: General Wrangel, immobilised in Hesse by the Imperials, called on him for help. But the Imperials and the Bavarians had placed their forces between the French and the Swedes. Leaving part of his infantry in Mainz, Turenne crossed the Moselle above Coblenz, crossed the Rhine into The Netherlands, descended towards Hesse and joined forces with the Swedes. On learning of the arrival of the French, the Imperials and the Bavarians under Erzherzog Leopold, who had not dared to attack the Swedes until then, had no choice but to withdraw in the face of the coalition forces. The Imperial general therefore chose to withdraw. However, Turenne, who only wanted passage, headed for Frankfurt and then crossed the Mein with Wrangel's Swedes. The Herzog von Bavaria took fright, had several bridges destroyed on the Danube and complained bitterly to the Emperor about the inaction of his general, Erzherzog Leopold. To the astonishment of the whole of Europe, the armies of France and Sweden entered Swabia and

---

4   Sun Tzu, *The Art of War*, p.107.
5   Sun Tzu, *The Art of War*, p.95.

THE BATTLE OF FRIBOURG 1644

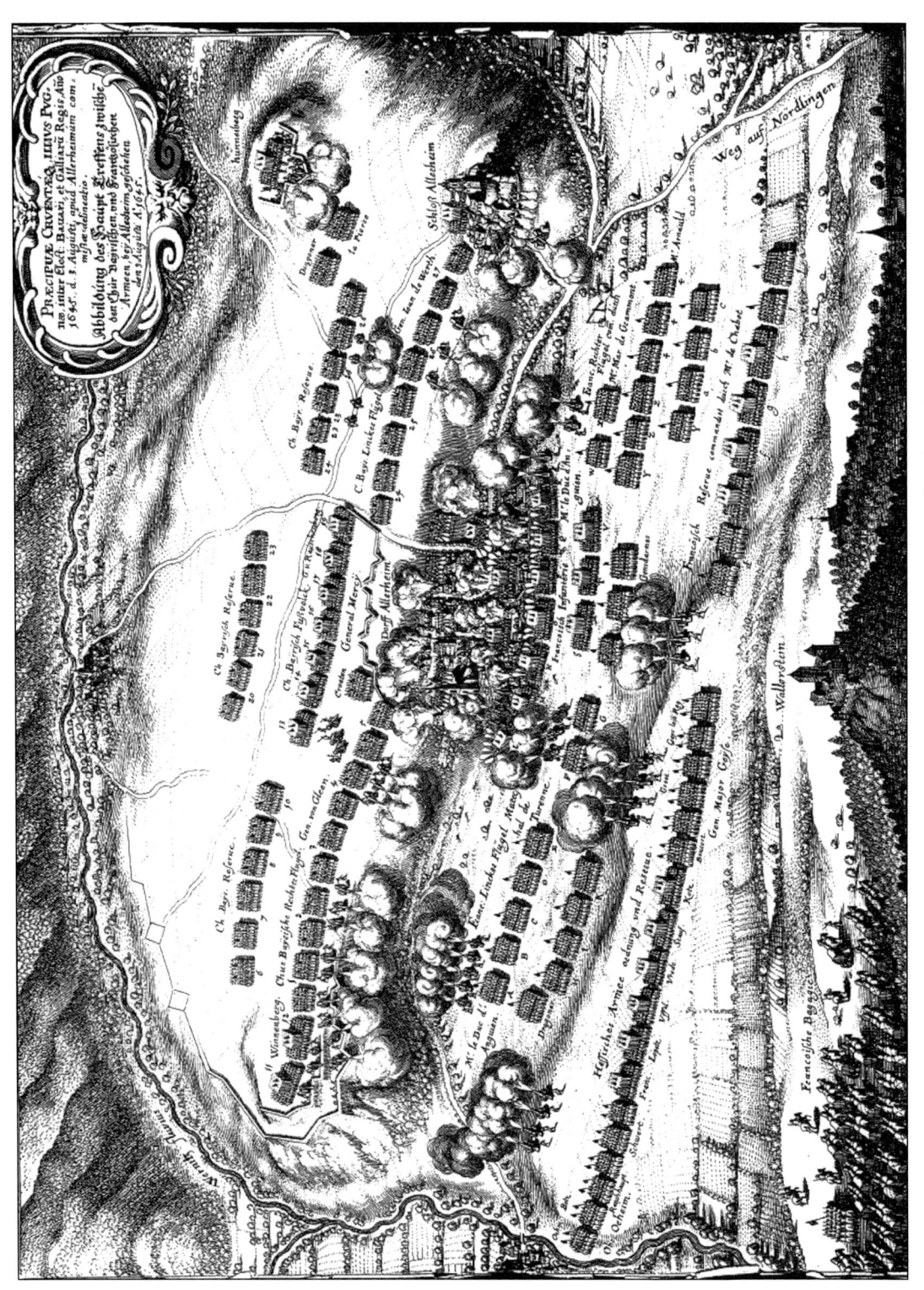

Battle of Alerheim, map from *Theatrum Europaeum*. (Public domain)

CONCLUSION

crossed the Danube. On 22 September, a siege was laid against Augsburg. The Emperor, who now feared that the Bavarians would defect, ordered Erzherzog Leopold to come to the city's aid. He arrived under Augsburg with a strong army, forcing the Franco-Swedish armies to withdraw. He then decided to wait until the allies ran out of fodder before attacking them and driving them back into Franconia. But Turenne and Wrangel had guessed his intentions. Believing Leopold's camp to be too strongly fortified, the allied generals pretended to want to attack. Then, leaving a curtain of horse to mask their movements, they crossed the river Lech and took Landsberg under the Erzherzog's nose. A masterstroke: Landsberg contained the Imperial stores – six weeks of provisions! Deprived of supplies, the Imperials went back to Austria to winter, thus separating themselves from their Bavarian ally. The consequences of this manoeuvre were incalculable: embittered, the Herzog von Bavaria decided to abandon the Emperor's side. On 14 March 1647, he signed an armistice with the French and Swedes.

The 1646 campaign was a brilliant one, enabling Mazarin and Louis XIV's France to achieve its objectives without having to fight a single battle, in the very spirit of Sun Tzu: 'Generally speaking, in war, the best policy is to take the State intact; annihilating it is only a second-best solution. Capturing the enemy army is better than destroying it; taking a battalion, a company or a squad of five men intact is better than destroying them.'[6]

In keeping with the spirit of the Chinese theorist, Turenne perfectly applied another of his principles:

> An army can be compared exactly to water, for just as a flowing stream avoids high ground and rushes towards low-lying areas, so an army avoids strength and strikes at weakness. And just as water follows the contours of the land, so an army, in order to achieve victory, adapts its action to the enemy's situation. And just as water has no stable form, there are no permanent conditions in war. Consequently, he who knows how to win by modifying his tactics according to the enemy's situation deserves to be considered divine.[7]

This is what Turenne did by bypassing the enemy forces blocking his path on the Rhine, moving north when his objective was the south, then moving back down towards Bavaria, taking several places in the process, then fixing the enemy with a screen of cavalry. From this perspective, it can be said that the manoeuvre proposed and implemented by Turenne to bypass the Mercy position at Fribourg was a first illustration of the 'Turenne method'.

In the end, the combination of d'Enghien and Turenne achieved an unexpected result against an excellent general, Mercy, and against a well entrenched army. The former contributed to this result through his decisiveness and doggedness, and the latter through his finesse and mastery of indirect style.

---

6 Sun Tzu, *The Art of War*, p.108.
7 Sun Tzu, *The Art of War*, p.137.

Colour Plate Commentaries

(by Stephen Ede-Borrett)

A. Maximilian von Bayern, 1620 (17 April 1573, Munich – 27 September 1651, Ingolstadt).
Maximilian I Herzog von Bayern from 1597, and then Elector from 1623 when the Electorate of the Palatine was transferred to him as a 'thank you' for his support against Elector Frederick of the Palatinate. Maximilian is shown in three-quarter armour, suitable for the field, over which is a blue scarf of Bavaria and just showing is the pendant of the Habsburg Order of the Golden Fleece (which, incidentally, still survives today). Watercolour by K.A. Wilke. (Lausanne, photo by the author.)

B. Johann von Werth (1591 – 16 January 1652).
In Imperial service, he had fought at the Battle of White Mountain in 1620. Shown here in three-quarter armour for the field with the red scarf of Imperial (and Spanish) service. While some high-ranking offers are portrayed in their portraits in gilded and decorated armour the majority wore plainer, and often more practical, armour in the field – like that of the rest of the armour either blackened at the forge or painted black. Watercolour by K.A. Wilke. (Lausanne, photo by the author.)

C. Bavarian Trumpeter.
Somewhat gaudily dressed, a not unusual affectation for trumpeters and kettledrummers, in clothing which reflects the Arms of Bavaria displayed on the banner of his trumpet. The same colours are displayed in the feathers of his hat. Note the falling sleeves on his doublet, which were almost universal for trumpeters during the seventeenth century and still appear on the State Coats of the trumpeters of the British Household Cavalry today. The use of a Coat of Arms on the trumpet banner would appear to have been customary in most armies, including the English, during the period. Watercolour by K.A. Wilke. (Lausanne, photo by the author.)

D. Imperial/Bavarian Kurassiers.
The left-hand figure shows the earlier close helmet which was rapidly falling out of fashion in favour of the more open 'lobster-pot' of the right-hand figure – the latter sacrificed some protection in favour of better visibility and

hearing. The standard is Bavarian, as is obvious from its design taken from the Coat of Arms of Bavaria (see illustration 003), the central design is shown at the left bottom, above that detail is the design for the reverse – a great many colours and standards of the German states carried differing designs on the obverse and the reverse. Watercolour by K.A. Wilke. (Lausanne, photo by the author.)

E. Louis II de Bourbon, Duc d'Enghien (Paris, 8 September 1621 – Fontainebleau, 11 November 1686).

Probably better known as The Prince de Condé, 'the Grande Condé' as he is known to the French (even if nowhere else), a title he succeeded to upon the death of his father in 1646. He was a soldier of exceptional abilities and fought throughout the numerous wars of the first part of the reign of Louis XIV – his last great battle was Seneffe on 11 August 1674. He was, however out of favour for a number of years having supported the Fronde. He is shown wearing blackened, three-quarter armour with the white scarf of the House of Bourbon over it, a colour reflected in the white feathers in his hat. His richly decorated saddlecloth appears to have not been unusual, even in the field and a number of similar saddlecloths survive throughout Europe. Watercolour by K.A. Wilke. (Lausanne, photo by the author.)

F. Henri de La Tour d'Auvergne (Sedan, 11 September 1611 – Salzbach, near Strasbourg, 27 July 1675).

Better known as *Maréchal* le Vicomte de Turenne, created *Maréchal* in 1643 and *Maréchal Général des Camps et Armées du Roi* in 1660. He started his military career in the Dutch Army but in 1630 turned to France. Turenne was an outstanding general officer who served France and was killed in battle at Salzbach when he was hit by a cannonball, on hearing the news Montecuccoli is reported to have said '*Il est mort aujourd'hui un homme qui faisait honneur à l'Homme*' (A man is dead today who did honour to Man). He was buried among the French Kings at St Denis and such was his reputation that when the Revolutionaries disinterred the bodies of the Kings, Turenne's tomb was left untouched. Turenne is dressed similarly to the Duc d'Enghien and the same comments apply. Note however the black and silver saddlecloth and pistol holsters – black and silver are the family livery colours and were also used for the troop standards of Turenne's Regiment of Horse, the clothing of that regiment's trumpeters, the colours of Turenne's Regiment of Foot and the clothing of the regiment's drummers.[1] Watercolour by K.A. Wilke. (Lausanne, photo by the author.)

G-H.
Based heavily on the engravings of French Infantry in *La Mareschal de Bataille* (Paris 1647), and the studies by Abraham Bosse, as well as other contemporary engravings these illustrations, although titled as 'French', are

---

[1] See other colour plates and Stephen Ede-Borrett, 'The Regiments of Turenne during the Thirty Years War and Franco-Spanish War, 1635–59' in *Arquebusier: The Journal of the Pike and Shot Society*, XXIV/III (London: The Pike and Shot Society, 2013).

also broadly indicative of the appearance of almost any of the infantry of the age, albeit there were some regional variations.

G. French infantry *c*. 1644.
Top, musketeer and a variety of types of headwear. Bottom from left to right: an officer, an ensign and a pikeman. The differing headwear is from musketeers in *La Mareschal de Bataille* and demonstrates that there was no uniformity in such items. The extravagant dress of the officer, his position indicated by his carrying of a half-pike, is usual in all armies and his expensive boots are another demonstration of his social position. The ensign, carrying a colour of the Gardes Françaises (probably of the Lieutenant Colonel's company), is dressed somewhat plainer than the previous figure but this would have been personal preference. The contemporary paintings of the Dutch *Schutterij* (Civic Guards) show ensigns were often the most flamboyantly dressed of the officers. Note the white scarf of both officers. The pikeman, carrying his helmet from some form of hook at his right rear is shown in a number of contemporary illustrations and paintings although evidence for such hooks is slight. Although armour for pikemen was being abandoned in some countries the evidence shows its continued use in the French Armies through to the last quarter of the century. Watercolour by K.A. Wilke. (Lausanne, photo by the author.)

H. French infantry *c*. 1644.
From left to right: an officer *c*. 1640, an officer *c*. 1645, an ensign and a fifer. The comments on the previous plate apply here but note the affectation of an 'arm scarf' on the right-hand officer – this appears on some contemporary illustrations but how practical it would be in the field is a matter of some conjecture (unless it was sewn and not actually tied). Watercolour by K.A. Wilke. (Lausanne, photo by the author.)

I. French infantry *c*. 1644.
From left to right: Pikeman, drummer from the *Gardes Françaises* and *petardier* (fireworker). All figures are, as in the previous illustrations, very fashionably dressed, albeit at a somewhat 'poorer' level than their officers. The annual replacement of clothing would have meant that most soldiers would have been broadly following 'fashions' albeit that decoration such as the ribbons at the bottom of the pikeman's breeches would have been added by the soldiers themselves (or more probably by the seamstresses amongst the camp followers). The figures are not wearing boots, which were far too expensive an item for the rank and file, but have additional stockings formed to emulate the boots of their 'betters'. The *petardier* with a pouch of grenades was recommended as useful to work with all pike units by George Monk, Duke of Albermarle among others; the concept was that *petardiers* would throw their grenades into the enemy pike body when it came to push of pike. Watercolour by K.A. Wilke. (Lausanne, photo by the author).

COLOUR PLATE COMMENTARIES

J. French cavalry:
From left to right: A *carabin* from Régiment de Condé cavalerie c. 1646, trumpeter from Régiment de Turenne cavalerie c. 1644. The *carabin* of the regiments of horse were to act as 'dragoons' in concert with their regiment in the way that English regiments of horse often had an integral dragoon company. These *carabins* were later taken from the regiments to be formed into two carabineer regiments which became the elite of the French line cavalry. The trumpeter (see comments on the plate of Turenne above) is wearing the black and white (silver) livery of d'Auvergne, although the trumpet banner displays the Royal Coat of Arms of France in place of the d'Auvergne Arms – perhaps a comment on Turenne's rank as *Maréchal*. Watercolour by K.A. Wilke. (Lausanne, photo by the author.)

K. Generic Dutch and German cavalry of the 1640s.
These troopers could equally well represent French horse of the period, although these latter had a reputation for being dressed somewhat more gaudily, as the later Parliamentarian general Sydenham Poyntz commented in 1635. The figures are all shown having drawn their swords to save precious moments after they fire their pistol and close to combat. Watercolour by K.A. Wilke. (Lausanne, photo by the author.)

L1.
Bavarian Colour from an old engraving depicting Mercy's death at Alerheim in 1645. This is probably the Colonel's Company Colours and shows the Bavarian Arms overlaid on the 'ragged cross of Burgundy', a common Habsburg device on Colours. The addition of the date of the Colours' presentation (manufacture?), 1640 in this case, is not uncommon on German colours of the seventeenth century. Note the two following colours are from the same regiment. Some of Mercy's regiments at Fribourg were also present at Alerheim – IR Gold, Mercy, Rouyer, Ruischenberg and Winterscheid. (Illustration by K.A. Wilke.)

L2.
Bavarian Colour from an old engraving depicting Mercy's death at Alerheim in 1645. Note the preceding and the following colours are from the same regiment. The blue and white lozenges of the Bavarian Arms are again overlaid with the Habsburg 'ragged cross' and the orb often displayed on Bavarian colours, traditionally representing a cross made from two tree branches with the 'ragged' showing where the side branches had been cut off – some earlier versions of the cross show these side branches with indications of the tree rings on their ends and the two arms as separate pieces. (Illustration by K.A. Wilke.)

L3.
Bavarian Colour from an old engraving depicting Mercy's death at Alerheim (1645). Note this and the preceding two colours are from the same regiment. The Bavarian 'origin' of this colour is indicated solely by the 'Bavarian blue' of the ragged cross. It is worthwhile noting that the Colours of a German

L4.

Bavarian Colour from an old engraving depicting Mercy's death at Alerheim (1645). Note this and the following two colours are from the same regiment. The colour displays Maximilian's cypher under the Electoral cap, as with the previous colour it is stylistically broadly similar to colours carried by the Bavarian Army over the next 200 years. (Illustration by K. A. Wilke.)

M1.

Bavarian Colour from an old engraving depicting Mercy's death at Alerheim in 1645. Based simply on the Bavarian Coat of Arms, this colour is virtually identical to that carried by the Bavarian Army in the Napoleonic Wars2. Note the preceding and the following colours are from the same regiment. (Illustration by K.A. Wilke.)

M2.

Bavarian Colour from an old engraving depicting Mercy's death at Alerheim (1645), Note this and the preceding two colours are from the same regiment. This is probably the Colonel's Company colours of the Regiment and the Madonna and Child at displayed at the centre, decorated throughout with extravagant gold 'flames'. The Madonna and Child device was common on the colours of Catholic German states during the Thirty Years' War and continued in use on Imperial Austrian Colours until the fall of the Empire in 1918. (Illustration by K.A. Wilke.)

M3.

Colour identified as Bavarian in the Stockholm Armémuseum in Stockholm, reference 833-VIII-I 8e delen. The motto *Sub Tuum Praesidium* translates as 'Under Thy Protection' and is from one of the most ancient of Marian hymns and prayers. Although traditionally identified as Bavarian the monogram of 'M A R' is confusing – the latter would normally refer to 'Rex' (King) which Maximilian was not,

M4.

French Standard of Turenne's Regiment of Horse. This is the Standard of the Colonel's troops of the Regiment and displays the Royal Coat of Arms in a similar form to that on the troops' trumpet banners (see plate 008) watercolour by K.A. Wilke. (Lausanne, author's photo.)

N1.

French Colour of a Weimarian Regiment of Foot. From an unidentified Weimarian regiment, this *ordonnance* colour is obviously, from its design, from a Colour issued after the Weimarians entered French service. The use of

---

2   Cf Rigo Le Plumet planche D3 & D7 (Paris ND [1980s]).

a semée of fleurs de lis on the Colours of a non-Royal regiment is unusual and may have been granted as a privilege. Watercolour by K.A. Wilke. (Lausanne, author's photo.)

N2. N3. N4. N5.
French Drapeau d'Ordonnance. These four Colours are instantly recognisable as French of a design that would essentially remain the same until the fall of the Monarchy in 1792 (even the Colours of the 1791 regulations, post Revolution are of this design). Although French regiments may have still had one colour per company in 1647 they had only carried two colours into the field from at least 1635, these were either two *Drapeau d'Ordonnace* or one *Drapeau Colonelle* and one *Drapeau d'Ordonnace* if the regiment were entitled to the white *Drapeau Colonelle* (a privilege by no means universal at the time).3 The colours of the cantons, and occasionally the device within that canton or the further division of it, served to make every *Drapeau d'Ordonnance* unique in design.

N2.
Mazarin-Italien Regiment of Foot. (Author's artwork)

N3.
Montausier Regiment of Foot (Author's artwork)

N4..
D'Enghien Regiment of Foot (Author's artwork)

N5.
La Reine-Mère Regiment of Foot, later La Couronne Regiment, although the colour of the cantons was changed to *bleu royal* at that time. (Author's artwork)

---

3 See Stéphane Thion, *French Armies of the Thirty Years' War*, 'Century of the Soldier no.117' (Warwick: Helion & Co, 2024).

Appendix I

Order of 10 October 1642[1]

Règlement fait par le Roy, pour le Logement & la Subsistance de ses Troupes pendant l'hiver prochain. 10 October 1642 in Ormeilles. (SHAT archives)

The King being obliged for the conservation of the troops of his armies, & for the relief of his people, to send his said troops during the next winter, in the cities, & main towns of his border provinces, & other neighbouring provinces; And wanting to provide that they recover in good condition to serve in the next campaign, & live in their quarters in good discipline & police, his Majesty ordered what follows.

I. In order to truly know the strength of the troops, both cavalry and infantry, the King wishes & intends that a review be carried out of them, by the commissioners in charge of them, at the first river crossing, or other strait that will be suitable for this purpose, after they have left the armies; from which review the said commissioners will send the ... to His Majesty, & ...; His Majesty very expressly forbidding them to dismiss any of their soldiers during the coming winter, as most have done in recent years.

II. His Majesty having resolved to reform all the companies of infantry which will be found by the aforementioned review lower than 20 men, the officers included, & all those of cavalry which will be lower than 30, also the officers included; wants that on the extracts of the aforementioned review a role of it will be drawn up, for this one seen by His Majesty, to be proceeded to the reform of these, according to the orders which it will send to the commissioners who will have the police force of the troops in their winter quarters.

III. All the French infantry regiments, except those which are specifically reserved by His Majesty, will be reduced to 20 companies; & among the companies which will be kept, those which are stronger will be preferred to the others.

---

1   SHAT archives 1642 A71-158.

IV. His Majesty having resolved to give more recruits neither to the infantry nor to the cavalry, & nevertheless wishing to give means to the chiefs of his troops to make them better than they have been in recent years, & to fill them with good soldiers; His Majesty understands, & orders that all his troops, both mounted and dismounted, will be paid by musters during the winter; & that even if at the said review, the companies are not complete, nevertheless all those of the infantry regiments will be paid at the first review on the basis of 56 men each, the royal companies for 150 men, those of *gendarmes* & *chevau-légers* for 60 men each, those of *carabins* for 50 men each, all officers included, in accordance with the statements that His Majesty will have sent, and the specific orders of the *intendants*, who will be appointed in each generality, or province, to take care of the subsistence and police of the troops; And if there were any company that was currently stronger than the said number, His Majesty wants it to be paid for all the men actually able to serve.

V. In the event that at the second muster there are not at least 40 men in each company, both of infantry and of *gendarmes*, *chevau-légers* and *carabins*, His Majesty forbids the said *intendants* to make the officers of the latter pay their allowances, because of the said watch; And if at the third time they do not have the said number of 56 men for the infantry company, 60 in those of *gendarmes* and *chevau-légers*, and 50 in those of *carabins*, His Majesty wishes and orders that they be dismissed; and that nevertheless before doing so, a statement of those who have failed to do so be sent to Him, in order to make His will known more expressly. After which the said *intendants* will dismiss the officers of the companies which will not be of the said number, and will make the soldiers of these companies enter the other companies of the same corps, which will have the said number; with a ban on leaving the service, on pain of life; and if any are so daring as to contravene this, they will have them arrested and punished in accordance with the severity of the present article. In addition, His Majesty wishes that the captains or officers commanding the companies who fail to make the said number, be forced to return all that they have received for the first and second watches of the winter quarter of their companies; & also to pay the same sum to those they have received for the said first & second watches, to which His Majesty has condemned them, & condemns them from now on as for then, to repair the damage to the State, & the service of His Majesty would receive from their negligence; & orders for the execution of this the aforementioned *intendants* to have the persons arrested, & seize the goods of the aforementioned captains, without them being able to be released, nor to have release, that after the actual payment in the hands of the treasurer of the extraordinary of the war, of the double of the sum which they will have received for the aforementioned musters.

VI. And so that the men of war know the good treatment which his Majesty has resolved to make them, it orders that it will be paid for each month of watch of 36 days to the captain of infantry 150 livres, amounting to 4 livres 3 sols 4 deniers per day; to the lieutenant 60 livres amounting to 33 sols 4 deniers per day; to the ensign 45 livres, amounting to 25 sols per day; to the two sergeants 43 livres 4 sols, which is to each 21 livres 12 sols per watch, & 12 sols per day; to three corporals 32 livres 8 sols, which is to each 10 livres 16 sols per watch, & 6 sols per day; to three lanspessadoes 27 livres, which is to each 9 livres per watch, & 5 sols per day; to four auxiliaries 36 livres, which is also to each 9 livres per watch, & 5 sols per day; & to 42 lanspessadoes 27 livres, which is to each 9 livres per watch, & 5 sols per day; & to 42 soldiers 302 livres 8 sols, which is to each 7 livres 4 sols per watch & 4 sols per day; in addition to the bread which will be provided at the expense of His Majesty to the sergeants & soldiers, the said appointments & salaries amounting to 696 livres per watch.

VII. The staff officers of each French infantry regiment will be paid the customary salary for each month of watch, also 36 days; & there will be a review of the said major officers, as well as of the others of the regiments, His Majesty wanting no major officer to be paid, if he is not currently in his charge, or if he does not have leave from His Majesty.

VIII. As for the *gendarmes*, *chevau-légers* & French carabins, they will also be paid a monthly watch, ordinary pay & salaries; but to enable the *chevau-légers* to subsist with order in the winter quarters, his Majesty, in consideration of the high cost of food, will have them pay a watch for each month of 30 days.

IX. The foreign troops both on foot and on horseback will also be paid by watches, according to their capitulation; & to put them on terms to satisfy it on their part, as His Majesty will be on his, the foreign regiments will be paid for as many companies, as there will be effective men in them, to make each company complete of the number carried by their capitulation.

X. The payments of all the troops will be made by half month's watch during the winter, according to the reviews, which will be carried out on the days that His Majesty will order.

XI. His Majesty considering that several army officers, who have companies in the cavalry and infantry, are paid the salaries of the said offices, & in addition to those of the captains of the said companies, to which being almost never present, those who command them have all the trouble, while the others do not perform any function, & this being unreasonable, His Majesty has ordered and orders that from now on during the campaign, any captain who is an officer in any army will only be paid half the captain's salary, and that the surplus will be given to the person commanding the company, to give him more means to maintain himself.

XII. All chiefs, officers and soldiers, both cavalry and infantry, shall be obliged to pay by mutual agreement for everything supplied to them, on pain of dismissal for the commanders and officers and life imprisonment for the soldiers. And to prevent food from being auctioned off to soldiers in garrison locations, His Majesty wishes the inhabitants of these locations to be obliged to supply them at the price of the last three contracts concluded before their entry into garrison; to which the *intendant*, and in his absence the commissioners for the conduct and police of the troops, will keep a careful watch; His Majesty wishes that if the inhabitants contravene this article, they will have them punished by fines, & such other penalties as the case may require; & if there is a contravention on the part of the people of war, they will make those who command the corps, & the conduct commissioners, responsible, having the payments of those who have caused or suffered to be caused by those of their company, any exaction or disorder, stopped, in order to use the funds to repair it, with a prohibition on the treasurers or their clerks, to pay them anything, on pain of striking off.

XIII. When the troops enter each garrison area, they will be placed in battle in the main square of the area, where they will be reviewed by the conduct commissioner, in the presence of...

[XIV. - XXI.]

XXII. Captains will be obliged to restore the arms of their companies to a state of service, & to have them all seen for their entire company, in the number mentioned in the fourth article of the present regulations, at the time of the second watch of the winter quarter; failing which the commissioners present at the said watch will have their allowances stopped at the hands of the treasurers, & the *intendants* will give their order to have them used to purchase weapons; & if the funds that will come from this are not sufficient to restore them to the condition, & to the number required for the whole company, the said commissioners will similarly have the captains' allowances stopped, & used for this purpose at the third watch.

XXIII. Captains of infantry will be obliged to have two-thirds of their soldiers armed with muskets, and one-third with pikes; and those of cavalry, to have theirs armed each with a cuirass, a pot, and two pistols, all in good condition.

XXIV. To maintain the soldiers in military discipline, & to ensure that the officers know their soldiers, & that their soldiers know them, His Majesty wishes that a guard be kept from 5 days to 5 days, by all infantry companies being at winter quarters in border towns, & other places; & that for the cavalry, that which will be in the frontier places be led or sent to war by those who will command it, as often as possible; & that that which will be elsewhere, be exercised every 8 days, in the most convenient place which will be found in the garrison place, or close to it; to which the *maréchals de camp* or others having authority over the troops, will carefully take charge.

XXV. And insofar as His Majesty has resolved not to make the fund of ten percent, for the watches which he will have paid to his infantry troops during the winter, His Majesty to distinguish those who serve well, from the others, will give 300 livres to each of the captains who have their companies complete, at the time of the payment of the second watch of the campaign, in addition to the allowances of this watch.

XXVI. And to prevent the abuse of the large number of horses with which the garrisons are overloaded during the winter, His Majesty orders that the *gendarme* may not have more than three horses during the winter, the *chevau-léger* not more than two, and the *carabin* three horses to two; &. if on entering the garrison they each have only one horse, they may not have more, unless they have purchased it with the knowledge and in the sight of the *commissaire à la conduite*, and have a certificate signed by him; & in any case the said number of horses may not be exceeded, failing which the *commissaire à la conduite* will be held accountable for the overload that the people may receive, in his own and private name.

XXVII. The captain of the *gendarmes* will have only 16 horses, both for personal service and for luggage, the lieutenant or sub-lieutenant 12, the ensign 8, the guidon 8, the *maréchal de logis* 6, the *fourriers* and petty officers each one; the *maître de camp* or colonel of a 16 horse *chevau-légers* regiment, the captain 12, the lieutenant 8, the cornet 6, the *maréchal de logis* 4, the petty officers each one; the sergeant major of a cavalry regiment, like a lieutenant, a provost marshal like a light horseman, his archers & the petty officers like a petty officer, the captain 12, the lieutenant 8, the cornet 6, the *maréchal de logis* 4, the petty officers each one. As for the cavalry staff, the colonel general of the cavalry may have up to 24 horses, the master-of-camp general 18, the provost general 2 horses, his archers, & the colonel's and the *maréchal de camp*'s men each one horse, the *maître de camp général* of the *carabins* 12 horses.

XXVIII. The infantry captain may have 4 horses in all, the lieutenant 3, the ensign 2. And as for the staff, each *maître de camp* may have as many horses as 2 captains, the lieutenant colonel & the sergeant major as a captain, the aide major as a lieutenant, the *maréchal de logis* as an ensign, the commissary of conduct as a captain, & the provost marshal as an ensign.

XXIX. No chief or officer, whether cavalry or infantry, may have the said number of horses unless he is present in the garrison. Nevertheless, His Majesty allows those absent with leave to keep in their quarters half the number of horses specified above, for which food will be provided in payment, as stated in the twelfth article of the present regulations, without those who have various charges being able to claim to have a greater number of horses than they are allowed above, for one of these; And if any of them are absent without leave, they may not have any valets or horses in the garrison, and the *intendants* and conduct commissioners are forbidden to tolerate this, or for the above order to be contravened, for any reason whatsoever and on any pretext whatsoever, on pain of being held accountable in their own private name.

XXX. Each chief, officer or soldier will have for utensils, a bed furnished with shrouds, and table linen, which his host may provide, according to his convenience, which the man-of-war will be obliged to make do with; & as for fire & candle, it will remain at the host's choice to give it to the man-of-war in common with him, or to provide him with wood, & the candle; namely to a captain of gendarmes per day, both for his person and for his train, one pound of candle; to a captain of infantry or cavalry, lieutenant, or second lieutenant of gendarmes, half a pound; to a lieutenant of infantry or cavalry, ensign, or guidon of *gendarmes*, captain of *carabins*, & cornet of *chevau-légers*, half a pound; to a captain of infantry or cavalry, ensign, or guidon of *gendarmes*, captain of *carabins*, & cornet of *chevau-légers*, half a pound. a lieutenant of infantry or cavalry, ensign, or guidon of *gendarmes*, captain of *carabins*, & cornet of *chevau-légers*, four candles of the twelve to the pound; to an ensign of infantry, a *maréchal de logis* of *gendarmes* & *chevau-légers*, lieutenant, & cornet of *carabins* three of the aforementioned weight; to a sergeant one of the same weight; to one or more soldiers housed together one of the sixteen to the pound; to a *gendarme, carabin, maréchal*, or *chevau-léger*, two of the twelve to the pound; to a *carabin* one of the same weight; & in places where it is difficult to find a candle, infantry soldiers will make do with the light of a lamp, either with their host, if they so wish, or separately at the choice of the host. As for wood, the captain of the *gendarmes* will be provided with 12 pieces, either logs, faggots or cottrets, part of one, part of the other, at the host's discretion; a captain of infantry or cavalry, and others treated as above, will also be provided with 6 pieces, without this equality being of any consequence in other respects; to a lieutenant of infantry, and other treaties as well, 4; to an ensign of infantry, and other treaties as well, 3; to a sergeant; to one or more soldiers in the same billet, one bundle or one cottret; to a *gendarme*, and other treaties as above, 2 pieces; to a *carabin*, one. And for major officers, both infantry and cavalry, the *maître de camp* or colonel will have two captains, the lieutenant colonel or sergeant major will have a captain, the aide major will have a lieutenant, the provost marshal and the *maréchal de logis* will have an ensign, the chaplain will have a sergeant, the conduct commissioner will have an infantry captain, and each of the *fourriers*, minor officers and archers, whether cavalry or infantry, will have a private soldier (...).

XXXIV. His Majesty understands & orders that during the winter in each regiment of French or foreign infantry, composed of 30 companies, at least 10 captains, 15 lieutenants & 15 ensigns will remain; in those of 20 companies 6 captains, 10 lieutenants & 10 ensigns, & in the others in proportion. For the cavalry, there must always be 2 officers present in each company, and the sergeants major, or their assistants, the provost marshals and the *archers*, both cavalry and infantry, must not be allowed to leave their posts in any way. Similarly no field officer of cavalry or infantry regiments may not be absent from his post without leave from His Majesty, countersigned by the Secretary of State responsible for the Department of War, and that all other officers who may have leave under this article must take it in writing from the person commanding the corps, endorsed by the conduct commissioner; failing which His Majesty forbids the treasurers to pay anything to the said absentees, on pain of removal from office and fourfold penalty. His Majesty desires that all the said officers absent with leave be obliged to return to their charges by the fifteenth of the month of February at the latest, to put themselves and their companies and troops in a good state of service; His Majesty forbidding the treasurers and their clerks to pay anything to those absent since the said fifteenth day of February, under the said penalties of striking off, and fourfold; & ordering the intendants to most graciously prevent any contravention of the present article. Requests & orders his Majesty to his *lieutenant général* in his armies, governors, *maréchals de camp*, *intendants* of justice, police & finance, employees in the said armies & provinces for the winter quarters of the troops, & all his other officers & subjects, to keep a close eye on the execution of the present regulation.

Appendix II

Extract from the order of 20 December 1643[1]

Regulation on the subject of the recruits of the infantry and cavalry troops of the King's Armies, and to prevent the Generals and Officers who command them from having various charges and other important points. 20 December 1643 (SHAT Archives)

> For the raising and arming of each recruit infantryman, 18 livres will be paid for the armies below and 24 livres for those of Italy and Catalonia.
>
> For the cavalry, the sum of 4,000 livres will be paid for the recruit of each company in any army, in accordance with the winter regulations of 18 October last.
>
> That the said fund for recruits will be distributed equally for each company, even though they may be stronger or weaker than one another. And each captain will be required to recruit from .... once he has received the levy, even if his company is already complete.
>
> Captains and officers will be obliged to arm their complete companies of 70 men each, armed for the infantry with two-thirds musketeers and one-third pikemen; and for the cavalry, each horseman in a pot, with breastplate in front and behind, and two pistols.
>
> That each cavalry company will have a Standard or the Cornet, and will march alone in the countryside... And any cavalry company with fewer than thirty men will not be able to have a Cornet.

---

1 SHD/SHAT A79-159

Appendix III

Typical deployment of an army in 1644

The *Maréchal de Bataille* was an office created by Louis XIII, probably shortly before his death. The *Maréchal de Bataille* was responsible for regulating the order of march and arranging the army in battle. He was assisted in this task by *sergents de bataille*. The Chevalier de La Valière was the first to be known by this title. He wrote a work entitled *Pratiques et maximes de la guerre*.[1] The aim of this treatise was to teach 'the duties of generals; the duties of all army officers; the order of marching, camping, fighting, attacking and defending places; surprising and attacking towns, districts or armies.'

At this time, an army on the march was divided into three corps: vanguard, battle and rearguard. In principle, marching troops kept 40 paces between squadrons and 25 paces between battalions. The positioning of a large army on a battlefield was a critical phase that had to take into account the terrain, its dimensions and the deployment of the enemy. According to La Valière:

> when you know the state of your army, and the number of battalions and squadrons that your troops can form, you must compose an order in which the troops can all support each other without confusion, and in such a way that one, being broken, does not overthrow the other, and that they fight on the widest possible front.

Then, according to his recommendations,

> the army is placed in three lines, the first of which is called the vanguard, the second the battle, which are roughly equal in strength, and the third the rearguard, when it is roughly equal in strength to the others, or the reserve corps, when it is much weaker. The infantry is placed in the middle, and the cavalry on the wings; the squadrons should be at least 80, 100 or 120 troopers, & 200 at most, and at present are only 3 deep. The battalions are of 6, 7 to 800 men, and 1,000 at the

---

1 François de la Valière, *Pratiques et maximes de la guerre* (Paris, 1666).

TYPICAL DEPLOYMENT OF AN ARMY IN 1644

most, of which the pikemen form the middle, and the musketeers the wings, and are 6 deep with the good troops, and 8 with the lesser ones.

The regiments of the *Gardes* and the *gendarmes* were placed in the middle of the line of battle, a 'fixed position,' allowing them to bolster and support the infantry, or to rally behind it if it was broken. *Carabins*, mounted riflemen, mounted guards and Croats were placed on the wings of the army. The vanguard and the battle must be 100 paces apart, while 200 paces must separate the battle from the rearguard.

> The squadrons and battalions of the battle are placed opposite the intervals left between those of the vanguard, so that the troops of the battle can pass between those of the vanguard to go to the enemy, and that those of the vanguard, being broken, can pass into the interval of those of the battle without falling on them. This gap is the width of the front of the squadron or battalion, which supports eight or ten paces more on each side. The battalions and squadrons of the rearguard are usually placed opposite the intervals of the troops in the battle. There are various ways of arranging these three corps, each of which has been given its own name, such as the cross, the chessboard, the cinquain, the fixain and several others that have no name. But the most common is the cross, and this is the tightest order, because the troops of the rearguard are opposite those of the vanguard.

Artillery – small-calibre falcons and hawks, medium and bastard culverins, large culverins of 15¼ pounds calibre or cannons of more than 33 pounds – generally cover the infantry front. Musketeers may be deployed in front, as skirmishers or *enfants perdus*, or on the flanks, in platoons of *commanded musketeers*, interspersed between cavalry squadrons.

Appendix IV

An army in battle in 1644

Jacques de Chastenet, seigneur de Puysegur, was captain and major in the Regiment of Piedmont from 1631. He was appointed *sergent de bataille* in 1644 and *Maréchal de Bataille* in 1648.

He wrote a work called *Instructions Militaires*, in which these are the provisions he recommended for putting an army into battle between 1644 and 1648:[1]

> How to place the vanguard on a line in plain country, with news of the enemy
>
> He who leads the right wing of the cavalry, being on the right, will open up as he marches; and he who leads the left in the same way, until they see that there is room for all the troops of the vanguard to be in the same line: and the regiment of infantry on the left hand, and that on the right, will then open from the cavalry; and so each regiment will take its place, the last being in the middle, and the artillery will be put between the battalions, or elsewhere where it is thought advisable to put them.
>
> Order to double the battle
>
> The Guards regiment will double to the right of the Gendarmes where the general's place will be, the Swiss to the left, the two less senior regiments, one to the right the other to the left, and so on until the last two which will be the two senior regiments. The older of the two will be on the right, the other on the left; the cavalry will double, that of the right on the right, that of the left on the left. Both cavalry and infantry brigades will be taken to make up the reserve troop, which will be separated from the battle by six to seven hundred paces, and the battle from the vanguard by three to four hundred. The baggage will be placed behind the reserve troop with sufficient guard.

---

1   Jacques de Chastenet de Puysegur, François Du Chesne, *Les Mémoires de messire Jacques de Chastenet, chevalier seigneur de Puysegur, Colonel du régiment de Piedmont, et lieutenant général des régiment de Piedmont, et règnes de Louis XIII et de Louis XIV. Given to the public by M. du Chesne, Councillor to the King in his Councils, Historiographer of France. Avec des Instructions militaires / Vicomte de Jacques de Chastenet Puysegur* (Amsterdam: Abraham Wolfgang, 1690)

Order of an army with the enemy on the right

The army will march by the flanks in two columns, and making to the right, will be in battle. At the head of the right-hand column will be the cavalry that is to cover it; the other wing, likewise the other column, and the baggage will march on the left.

If the enemies are on the left, the luggage will be placed on the right, with a sufficient number of musketeers to guard it.

The vanguard is always taken on the enemy's side; if they are on the left, the troops of the vanguard take it from the quarter, not on the march.

In a plain country, with the enemy in front of you, you can march the army in several lines, as would be an army in which there are sixty squadrons separated into four brigades to cover the wings of the two lines of infantry; march the fifteen squadrons which are to cover the right wing of the first line, and then march the other fifteen which cover the left wing; then the infantry in four lines : i.e. half of the first front line, as it is composed, or the whole of the first front line if you wish; and the second line of infantry afterwards in two lines, if you have the first there, and the cavalry of the second line in two lines, after the second line of your infantry, and the artillery in the intervals of the lines of infantry, where you deem it advisable to place them, and the baggage behind with sufficient guard for its safety.

Bibliography

Archival sources
SHAT archives SHD/SHAT Série A

Primary sources
Beaulieu, Sébastien de Pontault Sieur de, *Les Glorieuses Conquêtes de Louis le Grand, Roy de France et de Navarre* (Paris, 1694), tome 1
Bessé, Henri, Sieur de la Chapelle Milon, *Relation des Campagnes de Rocroi et Fribourg*, in Collection de Petits Classiques François (Paris: N. Delangle Editeur, 1826)
Du Bouchet, *Preuves de l'Histoire de l'Illustre Maison de Coligny* (Paris: Jean du Puis, 1662)
Bougeant, Guillaume Hyacynthe, *Histoire des Guerres et des Négociations qui précédèrent le traité de Westphalie* (Paris: Jean Mariette, 1727)
Champollion-Figeac, Aimé (ed.), *Mémoires de Mathieu Molé*, (Paris, Librarie de l'Histoire de France, 1856), tome 3
Puysegur, Jacques de Chastenet de, François Du Chesne, *Les Mémoires de Messire Jacques de Chastenet, chevalier seigneur de Puysegur, Colonel du régiment de Piedmont, et lieutenant général des régiment de Piedmont, et règnes de Louis XIII et de Louis XIV. Given to the public by M. du Chesne, Councillor to the King in his Councils, Historiographer of France. Avec des Instructions militaires / Vicomte de Jacques de Chastenet Puysegur* (Amsterdam: Abraham Wolfgang, 1690)
Chéruel, M. A. (ed.), *Lettres du Cardinal Mazarin pendant son ministère, recueillies et publiées par M.A. Chéruel* (Paris: M.A. Chéruel, 1872), vol.1
Chouppes, Aymar de, 'Mémoires du Marquis de Chouppes, Lieutenant Général des Armées du Roi' in *Mémoires du Marquis de Chouppes, lieutenant général des armées du Roi suivis des Mémoires Duc de Navailles et de la Valette pair et Maréchal de France et Gouverneur de Monseigneur le Duc de Chartres* (Paris: J. Techener, 1861)
Clermont, François de Paule de, 'Mémoires de François de Paule de Clermont, Marquis de Monglat' in *Collection des Mémoires relatifs à l'Histoire de France* (Paris: Petitot, 1825), tome 49
d'Erlach, Albert, *Mémoires Historiques Concernant M. le Général d'Erlach, Gouverneur de Brisach, Pays et Places en dépendants, Pour servir à l'histoire de la fameuse guerre de XXX ans & les regnes de Louis XIII & de Louis XIV* (Yverdon: 1784)

BIBLIOGRAPHY

Gramont, Antoine de, *Mémoires du Maréchal de Gramont* in Nouvelle collection des mémoires pour servir à l'histoire de France (Paris: Michaud et Poujoulat, 1839), troisième série, tome 7

Grimoard, Philippe-Henri de, *Collection des Lettres et Mémoires Trouvés dans les Porte-Feuilles du Maréchal de Turenne, pour servir de preuves et d'éclaircissements à une partie de l'histoire de Louis XIV, et particulièrement à celle des campagnes du général français* (Paris: Nyon, 1781)

Heilmann, Johann, *Die Feldzüge der Bayern in den Jahren 1643, 1644 und 1645 unter der befehlen des Feldmarschalls Franz Freiherr von Mercy* (Leipzig und Meissen: F.B. Goedsche 1851)

Heilmann, Johann, *Kriegsgeschichte von Bayern, Franken, Pfalz und Schwaben von 1506 bis 1651* (München: Literarisch-Artistische 1868)

Henault, Jean (ed.) *Tome Premier de l'Histoire de Nostre Temps Sous le Regne du Très-Chrestien Roy de France & de Navarre, Louis XIX es années 1643 & 1644 ou Tome Vingt-cinquiesme du Mercure François es Mesmes Années 1643 et 1644* (Paris, 1648), tome 2

Huffel C. van (ed.), *Documents Inédits Concernant l'Histoire de France, et particulièrement l'Alsace et son gouvernement, tirés des manuscrits de la bibliothèque du roi, des archives du royaume et autres dépôts* (Paris: Charles Hingray, 1840)

Letouf, Claude, *Mémoires et la vie de Messire Claude de Letouf, chevalier baron de Sirot, lieutenant général des camps et armées du Roi* (Paris: Claude Barbin, 1683)

Lostelneau, Sieur de, *Le Mareschal de Bataille, contenant le maniment des armes, les évolutionq, plusieurs bataillons tant contre l'Infanterie que contre la Cavalerie, divers ordres de batailles* (Paris, 1647)

Marichal, Paul (ed.), *Mémoires du Maréchal de Turenne publiés pour la Société de l'Histoire de France d'après le manuscrit autographe appartenant à M. le Marquis de Talhouët-Roy* (Paris: la Société de l'Histoire de France 1909)

Montecuccoli, Raimondo, *Mémoires de Montecuculi Generalissime des Troupes de l'Empereur, ou Principes de l'Art Militaire en général* (Paris: Muzier, 1712)

Richelieu, Armand J. du Plessis de, *Mémoires du Cardinal de Richelieu*, in Nouvelle Collection des Mémoires pour Servir à l'Histoire de France (Paris: Michaud & Poujoulat, 1838), tome 7

Ramsay, Andrew Michael, *Histoire du Vicomte de Turenne, Maréchal-Général des Armées du Roy* (The Hague: Jean Neaulme, 1736)

Renaudot, Théophraste, *Recueil des Gazettes et Nouvelles Ordinaires et Extraordinaires et autres relations des choses avenues toute l'année mille six cents quarante-quatre* (Paris, 1645)

Renaudot, Théophraste, 'Les avantages remportés par le Duc d'Enghien sur l'armée de Bavière, en deux sanglants combats donnés devant Fribourg les 3 et 5 de ce mois', in *Recueil des gazettes et nouvelles ordinaires et extraordinaires et autres relations des choses avenues toute l'année mille six cents quarante-quatre* (Paris, 1644)

Serres, Jean de, *Suitte de l'inventaire de l'histoire de France* (Paris, 1688), tome 2

Valière, François de la, *Pratiques et maximes de la guerre* (Paris, 1666)

Varennes, Olivier de (ed.), *Vingt-Troisiesme Tome du Mercure François, ou suitte de l'histoire de nostre temps, sous le regne du Très-Chrestien Roy de France & de Navarre Louis XIII. Es Années 1939 & 1940* (Paris, 1646)

Varillas, Antoine, *La Politique de la Maison d'Autriche* (Paris: Antoine Sommaville, 1658)

Secondary sources

Belhomme, Victor L. J. F., *Histoire de l'Infanterie en France* (Paris: Lavauzelle, 1893), tome 2

Bonaparte, Napoléon, *Précis des Guerres du Maréchal de Turenne*, https://gallica.bnf.fr/ark:/12148/bpt6k86480n.image

Chéruel, Adolphe, *Histoire de France pendant la minorité de Louis XIV* (Paris: Hachette, 1879).

Cust, Edward, *Lives of the warriors of the Thirty Years' War* (London: Murray, 1865), vol.2

Elster, Otto, *Die Piccolomini-Regimenter während des 30 Jährigen Krieges besonders das Kürassier-Regiment Alt-Piccolomini* (Wien: Verlag von Seidel & Sohn, 1903)

Guthrie, William P., *The Later Thirty Years War; From the battle of Wittstock to the Treaty of Westphalia* (Westport, Connecticut: Greenwood Press, 2003)

Lufft, August, *Die Schlachten bei Freiburg im August 1644* (Freiburg und Tübingen, 1882)

Noailles, Vicomte de, *Le Cardinal de la Valette, lieutenant général des armées du roi, 1635 à 1639* (Paris: Perrin et Cie , 1906)

d'Orléans, Henri, Duc d'Aumale, *Histoire des Princes de Condé Pendant les XVIe et XVIIe Siècles* (Paris: Calmann Lévy, 1886), tome 4

Roy, Jules, *Turenne, Sa Vie, les Institutions Militaires de son temps* (Paris: Hurtrel, 1884)

Schaufler, Hans-Helmut, *Die Schlacht bei Freiburg im Breisgau 1644* (Freiburg: Verlag Rombach, 1980)

Spring, Laurence *The Bavarian Army during the Thirty Years' War, 1618–1648* (Solihull: Helion & Co., 2017), Century of the Soldier 1618–1721 Series no. 15

Thion, Stéphane, *French Armies of the Thirty Years' War, 1618–1648* (Warwick: Helion & Co., 2024), Century of the Soldier 1618–1721 Series no. 117

Thion, Stéphane, *The Battle of Avins, 20 May 1635* (Auzielle: LRT Editions, 2011)

Other references

Sun Tzu, *The Art of War*, translated by Samuel B. Griffith (Oxford: Oxford University Press, 1963)

And with thanks to Gerhard Althaus and Sebastien Coels.

About the author

Stéphane Thion is a PhD in Human Sciences from Toulouse Capitole University. Passionate about history and strategy, and well-versed in research methods (he is currently Director of a Doctorate of Business Administration programme), he has been conducting research in the historical field for over 15 years. He is the author of several historical works on the 17th century: *French Armies of Thirty Years War*; *La bataille d'Avins 1635*; *La bataille de Rocroi*. He is also the author of the book *Le Soldat Lagide de Ptolémée Ier Sôter à Cléopâtre* and numerous articles in French magazines.

About the artist

Marco Capparoni is a artist and illustrator for wargames, fiction & nonfiction publishers, and private commissions. Specialising in history and military history, Marco's works also include natural history, portraiture, and book illustrations.

Other titles in the Century of the Soldier series

No 28 *Muscovy's Soldiers:* The Emergence of the Russian Army 1462–1689

No 29 *Home and Away:* The British Experience of War 1618–1721

No 30 *From Solebay to the Texel:* The Third Anglo-Dutch War, 1672–1674

No 31 *The Battle of Killiecrankie:* The First Jacobite Campaign, 1689–1691

No 32 *The Most Heavy Stroke:* The Battle of Roundway Down 1643

No 33 *The Cretan War (1645–1671):* The Venetian-Ottoman Struggle in the Mediterranean

No 34 *Peter the Great's Revenge:* The Russian Siege of Narva in 1704

No 35 *The Battle Of Glenshiel:* The Jacobite Rising in 1719

No 36 *Armies And Enemies Of Louis XIV: Volume 1* - Western Europe 1688–1714: France, Britain, Holland

No 37 *William III's Italian Ally:* Piedmont and the War of the League of Augsburg 1683–1697

No 38 *Wars and Soldiers in the Early Reign of Louis XIV: Volume 1* - The Army of the United Provinces of the Netherlands, 1660–1687

No 39 *In The Emperor's Service:* Wallenstein's Army, 1625–1634

No 40 *Charles XI's War:* The Scanian War Between Sweden and Denmark, 1675–1679

No 41 *The Armies and Wars of The Sun King 1643–1715: Volume 1:* The Guard of Louis XIV

No 42 *The Armies Of Philip IV Of Spain 1621–1665:* The Fight For European Supremacy

No 43 *Marlborough's Other Army:* The British Army and the Campaigns of the First Peninsular War, 1702–1712

No 44 *The Last Spanish Armada:* Britain And The War Of The Quadruple Alliance, 1718–1720

No 45 *Essential Agony:* The Battle of Dunbar 1650

No 46 *The Campaigns of Sir William Waller*

No 47 *Wars and Soldiers in the Early Reign of Louis XIV: Volume 2* - The Imperial Army, 1660–1689

No 48 *The Saxon Mars and His Force:* The Saxon Army During The Reign Of John George III 1680–1691

No 49 *The King's Irish:* The Royalist Anglo-Irish Foot of the English Civil War

No 50 *The Armies and Wars of the Sun King 1643-1715: Volume 2:* The Infantry of Louis XIV

No 51 *More Like Lions Than Men:* Sir William Brereton and the Cheshire Army of Parliament, 1642–46

No 52 *I Am Minded to Rise:* The Clothing, Weapons and Accoutrements of the Jacobites from 1689 to 1719

No 53 *The Perfection of Military Discipline:* The Plug Bayonet and the English Army 1660–1705

No 54 *The Lion From the North:* The Swedish Army During the Thirty Years War: Volume 1, 1618–1632

No 55 *Wars and Soldiers in the Early Reign of Louis XIV: Volume 3* - The Armies of the Ottoman Empire 1645–1718

No 56 *St. Ruth's Fatal Gamble:* The Battle of Aughrim 1691 and the Fall Of Jacobite Ireland

No 57 *Fighting for Liberty:* Argyll & Monmouth's Military Campaigns against the Government of King James, 1685

No 58 *The Armies and Wars of the Sun King 1643–1715: Volume 3:* The Cavalry of Louis XIV

No 59 *The Lion From the North:* The Swedish Army During the Thirty Years War: Volume 2, 1632–1648

No 60 *By Defeating My Enemies:* Charles XII of Sweden and the Great Northern War 1682–1721

No 61 *Despite Destruction, Misery and Privations..:* The Polish Army in Prussia during the war against Sweden 1626–1629

No 62 *The Armies of Sir Ralph Hopton:* The Royalist Armies of the West 1642–46

No 63 *Italy, Piedmont, and the War of the Spanish Succession 1701–1712*

No 64 *'Cannon played from the great fort':* Sieges in the Severn Valley during the English Civil War 1642–1646

No 65 *Carl Gustav Armfelt* and the Struggle for Finland During the Great Northern War

No 66 *In the Midst of the Kingdom:* The Royalist War Effort in the North Midlands 1642–1646

No 67 *The Anglo-Spanish War 1655–1660: Volume 1:* The War in the West Indies

No 68 *For a Parliament Freely Chosen:* The Rebellion of Sir George Booth, 1659

No 69 *The Bavarian Army During the Thirty Years War 1618–1648:* The Backbone of the Catholic League (revised second edition)

No 70 *The Armies and Wars of the Sun King 1643–1715: Volume 4:* The War of the Spanish Succession, Artillery, Engineers and Militias

No 71 *No Armour But Courage:* Colonel Sir George Lisle, 1615–1648 (Paperback reprint)

No 72 *The New Knights:* The Development of Cavalry in Western Europe, 1562–1700

No 73 *Cavalier Capital:* Oxford in the English Civil War 1642–1646 (Paperback reprint)

No 74 *The Anglo-Spanish War 1655–1660: Volume 2:* War in Jamaica

No 75 *The Perfect Militia:* The Stuart Trained Bands of England and Wales 1603–1642

No 76 *Wars and Soldiers in the Early Reign of Louis XIV: Volume 4* - The Armies of Spain 1659–1688

No 77 *The Battle of Nördlingen 1634:* The Bloody Fight Between Tercios and Brigades

No 78 *Wars and Soldiers in the Early Reign of Louis XIV: Volume 5* - The Portuguese Army 1659–1690

No 79 *We Came, We Saw, God Conquered:* The Polish-Lithuanian Commonwealth's military effort in the relief of Vienna, 1683

No 80 *Charles X's Wars: Volume 1* - Armies of the Swedish Deluge, 1655–1660

No 81 *Cromwell's Buffoon:* The Life and Career of the Regicide, Thomas Pride (Paperback reprint)

No 82 *The Colonial Ironsides:* English Expeditions under the Commonwealth and Protectorate, 1650–1660

No 83 *The English Garrison of Tangier:* Charles II's Colonial Venture in the Mediterranean, 1661–1684

No 84 *The Second Battle of Preston, 1715:* The Last Battle on English Soil

No 85 *To Settle the Crown:* Waging Civil War in Shropshire, 1642–1648 (Paperback reprint)

No 86 *A Very Gallant Gentleman:* Colonel Francis Thornhagh (1617–1648) and the Nottinghamshire Horse

No 87 *Charles X's Wars: Volume 2* - The Wars in the East, 1655–1657

No 88 *The Shōgun's Soldiers:* The Daily Life of Samurai and Soldiers in Edo Period Japan, 1603–1721 Volume 1

No 89 *Campaigns of the Eastern Association:* The Rise of Oliver Cromwell, 1642–1645

No 90 *The Army of Occupation in Ireland 1603–42:* Defending the Protestant Hegemony

No 91 *The Armies and Wars of the Sun King 1643–1715: Volume 5:* Buccaneers and Soldiers in the Americas

No 92 *New Worlds, Old Wars:* The Anglo-American Indian Wars 1607–1678

No 93 *Against the Deluge:* Polish and Lithuanian Armies During the War Against Sweden 1655–1660

No 94 *The Battle of Rocroi:* The Battle, the Myth and the Success of Propaganda

No 95 *The Shōgun's Soldiers:* The Daily Life of Samurai and Soldiers in Edo Period Japan, 1603–1721 Volume 2

No 96 *Science of Arms: the Art of War in the Century of the Soldier 1672–1699: Volume 1:* Preparation for War and the Infantry

No 97 *Charles X's Wars: Volume 3* - The Danish Wars 1657–1660

No 98 *Wars and Soldiers in the Early Reign of Louis XIV: Volume 6* - Armies of the Italian States 1660–1690 Part 1

No 99 *Dragoons and Dragoon Operations in the British Civil Wars, 1638–1653*

No 100 *Wars and Soldiers in the Early Reign of Louis XIV: Volume 6* - Armies of the Italian States 1660–1690 Part 2

No 101 *1648 and All That:* The Scottish Invasions of England, 1648 and 1651: Proceedings of the 2022 Helion and Company 'Century of the Soldier' Conference

No 102 *John Hampden and the Battle of Chalgrove:* The Political and Military Life of Hampden and his Legacy

No 103 *The City Horse:* London's militia cavalry during the English Civil War, 1642–1660

No 104 *The Battle of Lützen 1632:* A Reassessment

No 105 *Monmouth's First Rebellion:* The Later Covenanter Risings, 1660–1685

No 106 *Raw Generals and Green Soldiers:* Catholic Armies in Ireland 1641–1643

No 107 *Polish, Lithuanian and Cossack armies versus the might of the Ottoman Empire*

No 108 *Soldiers and Civilians, Transport and Provisions:* Early Modern Military Logistics and Supply Systems During The British Civil Wars, 1638-1653

No 109 *Batter their walls, gates and Forts:* The Proceedings of the 2022 English Civil War Fortress Symposium

No 110 *The Town Well Fortified:* The Fortresses of the Civil Wars in Britain, 1639-1660

No 111 *Crucible of the Jacobite '15:* The Battle of Sheriffmuir 1715

No 112 *Charles XII's Karoliners Volume 2* - The Swedish Cavalry of the Great Northern War 1700-1721

No 113 *Wars and Soldiers in the Early Reign of Louis XIV: Volume 7* - Armies of the German States 1655–1690 Part 1

No 114 *The First British Army 1624–1628:* The Army of the Duke of Buckingham (Revised Edition)

No 115 *The Army of Transylvania (1613–1690):* War and military organization from the 'golden age' of the Principality to the Habsburg conquest

No 116 *The Army of the Manchu Empire:* The Conquest Army and the Imperial Army of Qing China, 1600–1727

No 117 *French Armies of The Thirty Years' War 1618–48*

No 118 *Soldiers' Clothing of the Early 17th Century:* Britain and Western Europe 1618–1660

No 119 *Novelty and Change:* Proceedings of the 2023 Helion and company 'Century of the Soldier' Conference

No 120 *Peter The Great's Disastrous Defeat:* The Swedish Victory at Narva, 1700

No 121 *The Battle of Fribourg 1644:* Eughien and Turenne at War

SERIES SPECIALS:

No 1 *Charles XII's Karoliners: Volume 1:* The Swedish Infantry & Artillery of the Great Northern War 1700–1721